pathways

A Guide for Energizing &
Enriching Band, Orchestra,
& Choral Programs

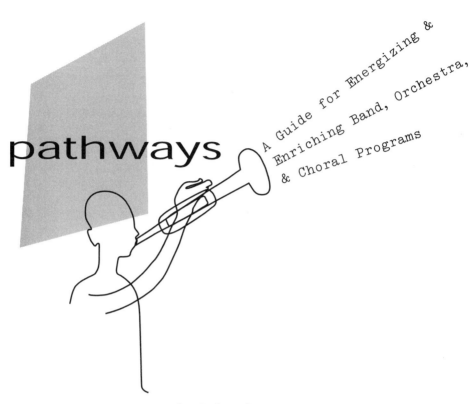

pathways

A Guide for Energizing & Enriching Band, Orchestra, & Choral Programs

Joseph Alsobrook foreword by Tim Lautzenheiser

GIA Publications, Inc.
Chicago

For Mic-Mic and The Bub

Pathways Joseph Alsobrook

Jacket design and illustration by Yolanda Durán
Book design and illustrations by Yolanda Durán

G-5641
ISBN: 1-57999-134-3
Copyright © 2002 GIA Publications, Inc.
7404 S. Mason Ave., Chicago, IL 60638
www.giamusic.com
Printed in the United States of America.

Table of Contents

Acknowledgements vii

Foreword by Tim Lautzenheiser ix

Prelude xi

Introduction xix

The Gift of Love 1

The Gift of Attention .29

The Gift of Accomplishment 55

The Gift of Boundaries 155

The Gift of Fun 181

Crossroads 209

Endnotes 217

About the Author 226

Acknowledgments

This book is a result of years of trial-and-error practice, the wisdom of many outstanding music educators, innumerable hours of reading and research, and infinite lessons from my students. Without the support and inspiration of several very special people, however, it would never have been possible.

To the many talented directors that I have had the pleasure of working with over the years, thank you for sharing your expertise. Most of the ideas in this text are lessons learned from observing you in action...on the front lines of music education.

I use not only all the brains I have, but all I can borrow.

- Woodrow Wilson -

To my father, thank you for leading me to music. I am certain that music is my calling. I am also certain that I would have missed it without your guidance.

To my mother, part master teacher, part editor, part leprechaun, thank you for the hours and hours of help with this book, for enduring the first manuscript, and for your never-ending encouragement...just as you always have in all my undertakings.

To my grandparents, thank you for your endless

support, for all the concerts you took me to as a child, and for always knowing just the right songs to sing and stories to tell.

To my sons Micah and Jordan, thank you for enduring the creation of this book...especially all of those hours that you let me work when you really didn't want to. It has been said that music fuels the spirit...for me, it is the two of you.

And to my wife Connie, thank you for always keeping me on the right track, for leading me to all the words that I could not find, for willingly sharing your amazing wisdom, and for sacrificing so much. Giving comes as naturally to you as breathing...countless children have been blessed by the abundant love that lives in your heart.

Foreword Tim Lautzenheiser

Every now and then someone brings forth a unique bit of wisdom that has the ability to positively impact the lives of countless people. I suspect, for the most part, much of this enlightenment is never recorded or shared with others, but is the result of a spontaneous epiphany generated "at the moment." However (and unfortunately), there is little evidence, except for some personal memories, that anything extraordinary ever happened. Joe Alsobrook brings to us a book of such wisdoms, *Pathways,* certain to open the minds of all who are committed to excellence.

In his writings, Joe has gone beyond the theoretical aspects of *masterful teaching* by giving us clear and concise blueprints for effective and efficient learning. His references come from those who have "walked the pathway," and his embellishment of their thoughts and notions allow all of us to access a higher level of understanding.

Pathways is a compilation of great ideas integrated with a series of pragmatic recipes for success. This is not another "tricks of the trade" manual, but rather a profound perspective of *what we do* and, more impor- tantly, *why we do it.* While it is written specifically for the discipline of music, it is applicable to every area of teaching, and it should be required reading for anyone working with our young minds of today.

I applaud Joe Alsobrook for his extraordinary insight. He has given all of us a gift that will improve our students, our schools, and ourselves!

Prelude

Year after year it's the same old thing. As music educators, we work diligently to attract students, bend over backwards to teach them as much as possible, live on very little sleep to keep up with the schedule, spend hours waiting on their rides, and go out of our way to help them in any way that we can. Then it happens. The little darling for whom we sacrificed so much, the young inspiring musician for whom we had so many plans...QUITS(!)...and without even saying goodbye. Has this happened to you? If not, you're doing something unbelievably right...so keep it up. If it has, however, welcome to the club.

Throughout the first few years of my teaching career, I tried everything I could think of to keep students in my program. I mean everything. From free days to french fries, we did it all. And what happened when all was said and done? Well, I think this will give you the idea: "Great class, Mr. A; I really enjoyed it. I hope to see you again sometime. By the way, do you know anyone who might want to buy my trumpet?" Get the picture? When the party was over, so was their music education.

Unfortunately, this was not just happening in one particular class, it was the story throughout the entire program. Students were leaving for all sorts of reasons.

Some I could understand and some I couldn't. But that never really mattered. Quitting is quitting, and once students are gone, the chances of them changing their minds and returning are slim at best.

As you might have guessed, I eventually fell victim to the notorious "I don't care" attitude. I saw nothing, absolutely nothing, wrong with my teaching or the way I was running the program. The students were wrong. If they didn't want to be a part of the program, that was fine. It was their loss.

But it really wasn't. I was the one who was losing. Music was my calling, and when students dropped out for whatever reason, I didn't take it lightly. The students who scratched music off of their schedules, and probably out of their lives, just might have been the next Wynton Marsalis or Andrea Bochelli. The very reason I became a music educator in the first place was walking out on me...and in no small numbers.

To make matters even worse, I had big plans. The way I saw it, if 200 students started in the sixth grade, and I continued to recruit at least this many in each year that followed, by the time the first sixth grade class got to be seniors, there would be approximately 750 students in the high school and somewhere around 1200 in the total program. Whoa! Was I dreaming or what? After just two semesters, did things go as planned? Not even close. You guessed it. Same story...different year. Things were out of control and a solution to this problem had to be found. My mission was clear, and thus began the quest that led to the inspiration for writing this book.

Make no mistake about it; student retention is most definitely an issue that all music educators need to be concerned about. Music is eminently beneficial for students—the values of music are substantial and significant—and nurturing musicianship "comprehensively" is a progressive process that requires keeping students from year to year. Without students, you also have no support. You get very little funds to run your program and a thriving booster organization is out of the question. In this day and age of budget crunches, you cannot afford to let your membership decline or even run in place. In short, without students, you run the very real risk of losing your program entirely.

Anyway, as I began hunting for answers, it didn't take long to realize that students who stayed in music programs did so for many reasons. For example, programs rich in tradition and programs that provide frequent opportunities to travel are often very successful at keeping students. Programs under the direction of truly inspiring musicians also do quite well. Indeed, all of these factors contribute, but only to a certain degree. A single, magical answer that would solve the problem completely was just not appearing. What I did find, however, were some very real similarities between thriving music programs and master teachers. And interestingly enough, they were not necessarily musical at all.

Friends, I have good news. The solution to this seemingly never-ending problem can be found in every rehearsal room on the planet. It lies within the expressions on your students' faces, it's reflected in the nature of your students' actions, and most of all, it's implicit in just about every word that comes out of your students' mouths. And when you focus on learning to understand rather than always trying to be understood, the answer becomes perfectly clear.

Here we go. This can have a tremendous impact on your students' futures as well as your career as a music educator, so read it twice.

> The key to a thriving music program and a truly meaningful career as a school band, orchestra, or choir director is to give your students what they want most.

The combination of giving students what they want (need!) most and the natural, enriching effects of music is a potent formula for success. These "gifts" are irresistible magnets that attract and sustain interest like nothing else. They virtually guarantee the presence of happy, motivated, and musical students year after year. Students come to school everyday in search of these things, and when they find them, you can be certain they will want to come back for more. Yes...

. . . they will get up at ridiculous hours to attend rehearsals.

. . . they will show up for every performance.

. . . they will obtain each and every item that is required.

. . . they will listen to your every word as if Toscannini himself were speaking.

. . . they will conduct themselves in a manner that is pleasing to you.

. . . they will genuinely try to accommodate all of your requests.

. . . they will meet deadlines.

. . . they will practice their music.

...but only if they are getting what
they want most in return.

Just what is it that students want most? For starters, it's not what you're probably thinking. It has nothing to do with parties, free time, or whirlwind excursions to distant lands. Nor does it have anything to do with a three-tiered, gold-plated trophy. Regardless of what we may think sometimes, students are living, breathing, thinking, and feeling creatures who want the same things that you and I and most of the planet want. There are *fundamental aspirations* that we all require, and if your program fulfills them, students will come, students will grow, and students will stay.

Now for some even better news. When students get what they want most, the "musical flame" keeps burning and *learning potential is monumental*—students become more absorbed in making music than you ever thought was possible. Furthermore, parents are thrilled because their children are excited and learning. And when children are learning and parents are happy, obviously your administration will be as well. It's a win-win-win situation.

This brings us to you—the teacher, motivator, musician,

musical authority, peace keeper, judge, jury, counselor, ally, and supporter, with the power to make all of this come true. Be confident in the fact that the *gifts of giving are many.* Benevolence is a give-and-take proposition; when you focus on giving, you get so much in return. Frustration is replaced with the satisfaction that comes from enabling others to succeed, days of strain and struggle are virtually nonexistent, and frequent boosts of self-confidence confirm one of life's most important decisions. You were right! Music education is a worthy profession filled with meaningful purpose and abundant rewards.

Introduction

Have you ever given thought to the question, "What do you hope people will say about you when you're gone?" Better yet, author Steven Levine asks, "If you had an hour to live and could make only one phone call, who would you call, what would you say, and why are you waiting?" Don't you hate these questions? They make you really think about your life...where you've been, where you are today, and where you'll be tomorrow. For many of us, these aren't always the most comforting thoughts. As annoying as they may be, however, thought-provoking queries awaken us to the directions that we have chosen for our lives. The same holds true in regards to the directions we take with our students. Approaching music education with firm answers to questions such as the following is paramount to achieving genuine success:

Why do I do what I do?

What do I really want my students to learn?

When my students leave, what will they take with them?

Will the things that students learn in my classes enrich their lives?

The purpose of this book is to help you formulate answers for these types of questions and to energize **the great director within you.** More specifically, this text proposes *a giving approach to music education.* The multitude of thoughts, ideas, and strategies on the pages that follow are intended to help give students the absolutely indispensable things that they want (need!) most. These gifts are pathways that lead to musical and personal enrichment for both students and directors. Each gift plays an important role in bringing out the best in others, as well as making your career as a band, orchestra, or choir director rich and meaningful.

It is important to note that a key premise of this text is that it takes far more than musical knowledge alone to be an effective band, orchestra, or choir director. Thus, teaching specific musical concepts such as singing with a beautiful tone, matching pitch, developing technique, or shaping expressive phrases is not the intent here. Many great resources by many great musicians already exist for such matters. In contrast, *Pathways is a collection of practical and creative options that will help you to:*

Set the mental, physical, and emotional stage for truly exceptional musical teaching and learning experiences.

> Sustain the natural attraction that all children have for making music.

These options are presented in five major sections, each targeting an essential gift that *all* students need to receive. Please do not interpret the order in which these gifts are cast as an order of importance. Each gift is indispensable and mutually reinforcing. It is the combination of all of these gifts and the natural, enriching effects of music that is the real key to unlocking great interest and achievement in any band, orchestra, or choral program.

One more thing. True to the nature and essence of giving, one of the most significant values of this text lies in its simplicity. By considering each section as an area of concentration, a powerful yet far from complex formula for musical and personal growth begins to emerge. Work on elevating the amount of energy you devote to each area and watch the magic happen.

Good luck and God bless!

The quotes contained in this book were collected over a period of years from a variety of sources. In some cases the authors are unknown, and I would like this to be an acknowledgment of appreciation for their words of wisdom.

the gift of love

> We can do no great things on this earth.
>
> We can only do small things with great love.
>
> -Mother Teresa-

The desire to be loved and accepted is something that everyone shares in common. In the context of teaching, making your students feel welcome and important is an essential first step in building long-term, cooperative relationships. This does not mean that everything that comes out of your mouth must be sugary and sweet. Messages of respect, appreciation, and compassion are as inherent in your actions as they are in your words.

2

When problems arise, replace anger with action.

Rage and reason do not mix. Sudden bursts of anger convey that you have lost control, turn students off, and destroy learning potential by creating an atmosphere of tension. Use a pointed tone when necessary to command student attention, but always remain in control. The common ground between all effective classroom management strategies is to remain calm while initiating positive action. Not only will this keep you sane, but it will send a message of respect while providing students with a model of how to deal with stressful circumstances in a peaceful, rational fashion. Here are some specific examples of how trying scenarios can be turned around with *action,* not *anger:*

Scenario

The entire class is unfocused and talkative.

Positive Actions

■ Make sure the task at hand is meaningful for the entire group. Try moving to a section of the piece you are working on that will engage everyone. If the rehearsal becomes unfocused each time you work on a particular piece, chances are good that the selection is either too difficult or too easy.

■ Ask for positive action. For example, instead of saying, "Stop interrupting me," ask students to raise their hands and be recognized before they speak. [1]

■ Be everywhere in the classroom. Structure space so you can move around and get close to every student. Most discipline problems are a direct result of too much distance between the student and the teacher.

> I like to compare the teacher to a wood-burning stove: Just as the warmth from the stove decreases with our distance from it, the effect of the teacher decreases as his or her distance from students increases. [2]
>
> -Judith Delzell-

<u>**3**</u>

■ Teach your students that after a five-second count-down with your fingers, or similar signal, they are to immediately begin playing or singing a certain note. Use this procedure as needed to capture or restore attention. If students are really unfocused, you can sustain their attention by moving up and/or down from the initial note using hand signals.

■ As a last resort, stop what you are doing, select a short passage from the material you are working on, and give an impromptu performance test. Make it per-fectly clear that any interruption will result in a zero.

4

It often shows a fine command of the language to say nothing.

Scenario

The rehearsal is going nowhere fast.

Positive Actions

■ Give students a two-minute "time-out."
"You have two minutes to practice the first twenty-four measures of this song. Your time starts right now."

■ Don't try to do everything yourself. Encourage students to use their good judgment and make independent musical decisions that will help accomplish the task(s) at hand.

■ Clarify your goals.
"OK, we're in pretty deep here, so let's break things down.

This time keep your attention exclusively on maintaining tempo between the letters B and C. See if you can pinpoint exactly where we are speeding up."

■ Become Mr. or Mrs. Enthusiasm. The transformational power of positive energy is highly underrated. *"Tenors, great job!" "Wow, that was way cool!"*

■ Switch gears by changing songs or moving to a different section of the piece you are working on. Devise a specific plan of attack for working the trouble spot(s) before the next rehearsal.

■ Take a "seventh-inning stretch."

5

There is a notable difference between "talking" and "interaction."

Learn all of your students' names and use them when addressing students.

Few things can turn a student off faster than a teacher who doesn't take the time to learn his/her name. Insist that your students learn each other's names as well. You can't make great music in a group of strangers and no child wants to be known as "soprano in the blue shirt" or "last chair clarinet."

Use an "adult voice," not a "parent voice," when addressing disciplinary issues.

Avoid common, judgmental, evaluative comments that instantly put students in a defensive mode:

You (shouldn't) should do that.
It's wrong (right) to do....
That's (stupid, immature, out of line, ridiculous).
Life's not fair. Get busy.
You are (good, bad, beautiful, worthless).
You do as I say.
If you weren't so..., this wouldn't happen to you.

In place of these statements, use more neutral comments or questions such as:

In what ways could this be resolved?
I would like to recommend...
What are your choices in this situation?
I am comfortable (uncomfortable) with...
Options that could be considered are...
For me to be comfortable, I need the following things to occur...
These are the consequences of that choice/action...
We agree to disagree.

By addressing unpleasant situations with a non-judgmental, factual tone, you will quickly realize that students respond much more willingly to your requests. At the same time, students quickly realize that you are on their side and that your ultimate mission is to simply come up with a workable solution to the problem. [3]

Put your students first.

The music director is the CEO of the program;

he/she "steers the ship." In order to teach comprehensive musicianship to each student, the director must steer the program towards being student centered rather than program centered. *Enriching lives through music...one student at a time,* for example, describes a program focused on helping each and every student discover the many ways that music can be a lifelong source of growth and enjoyment. In this type of program, success is measured one student at a time, not one trophy at a time.

Unfortunately, it is so easy to head in the opposite direction and become obsessed with contests. It has become commonplace to structure and operate an entire program around the sole purpose of achieving superior ratings. The quest for "ones" has replaced the mission to provide students with a unique form of knowledge, growth, and optimal experience. This is the tail wagging the dog! A hunt for first divisions alone is more often than not a self-serving, ego-building mission by the director disguised as motivation for high musical achievement. In *The Seat of the Soul,* Gary Zukav reinforces this view:

To compete means to strive for something in company or together, to aim at something, to try to reach something, to seek after something with others. If the something that you aim for is prestige or notice or a gold medal instead of a tin medal, it is your personality that is motivating the competition. You are striving to empower yourself at the expense of others, to assert your superiority over another, or over other human beings. You are striving for external power. By striving for this reward and that reward, you ask the world to assess and acknowledge your value before you can value yourself. You place your sense of self worth in the hands of others. You have no power even if you win every gold medal that the world can produce. [4]

8

Contrary to popular belief, sacrificing everything for superior ratings is not the way to keep students interested in music-making, nor is it the magic motivator for high levels of retention and musicianship. As Will Schmid, former President of MENC remarks, "Spending week after week drilling notes on festival pieces just to achieve the 'I' rating is truly deadening to students." [5] Oftentimes the only thing students really remember about this experience is the beating they took to get there. Furthermore, if preparation for competition consumes most of a student's time and efforts in a music program, it can destroy interest in music-making for years to come. A comment by Eugene Corporon seems appropriate here:

We try to recruit students to play in the campus band, which is a non-major group. We run into some kids who own Buffet clarinets who play well. They say, "I don't ever want to do anything in music again, I hate it." You think, my God, after four years of high school, that's what's happened to them, they hate music? They feel abused and they feel used up. You think the mark of a great music program is that some-one would say, "You know I want to stay in music the rest of my life...I just can't do without it! I may not make my living at it, but I had such a great experience with it I want it to be part of my life." [6]

True motivation to continue and increase musician-ship results from the feelings that are created within ourselves when we are engaged in artistic music-making. These values arise when students engage in compelling musical challenges that are in balanced relation to their current level of musicianship, *not* to the contest list. Although there are always several works on state contest lists that would be appropriate, oftentimes directors ignore these and seek "safe" composi-tions, which are boring to students. Another trend is to select obscure works that "no one knows" over proven classics. Why? To secure the best odds for a top rating, not the best chances for genuine musical growth.

The message here is *not* to abandon contests, but to keep them in perspective. Superior ratings can, and most likely will, be a natural occurrence in programs focused on helping each student develop his/her musicianship as deeply as possible. When competitive events are approached in a giving manner and represent just one component of a balanced performance calendar, they can provide very positive and constructive learning experiences. As Eldon Janzen points out, "Certainly it is difficult to be critical of a superior performance. High achievement is a goal of the American way. The democratic process encourages complete freedom to become the best." [7] Furthermore, the "internal goods" of music result from learning to make and listen for music well—from the deliberate and sustained pursuit of musical competency, proficiency, and expertise. To pursue musical excellence is to pursue self-growth, constructive knowledge, and enjoyment.[8] The key is to refrain from organizing your program and basing your entire worth as a music director solely on the situated opinion of others.

Here are some suggestions for keeping competition healthy and productive:

■ Use contests as motivation to *uncover* all of the layers of information presented by exemplary musical works.

■ Inform students and parents that success at contests is an outgrowth of learning and not an end in itself.[9]

■ Think of contests as opportunities to receive constructive ideas for making your next performance even better. Explain to your students how these events allow them to perform for fellow musicians who have the knowledge and experience to really appreciate their efforts.

■ Schedule time after all competitions to reflect upon the achievement of musical goals rather than the results of the contest.[10]

11

■ Stress the fact that you have no control over the outcome of any group except your own. Thus, the real contest is against yourself. Setting goals, and then reaching them, is the ultimate measure of success.

■ Encourage students to participate in solo/ensemble festivals, honor groups, etc. These events provide competition to those who need it.[11]

■ Consistently low ratings and poor scores indicate that it's time to re-examine your methods and take corrective action. The values of music-making arise when music is made *well*. Excuses are easily made, but real solutions will not appear until you are willing to make progressive changes.

Student-centered programs thrive on helping each individual achieve high levels of musicianship, thus boosting the opportunity to experience the significant values that music has to share. For the director, focusing on individual musical achievement as opposed to top ratings provides deep, personal satisfaction that lasts a lifetime...not just a few minutes of "one-der-ful-ness."

Music has been an important part of academic study throughout the civilized world, since Aristotle and Plato. It was never intended to be a public relations vehicle, a supporter of school spirit, a competitive vehicle to support and enlarge the interscholastic athletic program, or designed to keep youth out of trouble. It was simply an intellectual discipline that fed both the mind and the spirit.

-Kenneth Raessler
(Music Chair, Texas
Christian University)-

Go with the flow.

Before you get frustrated in rehearsal because things aren't going exactly as you had planned, take a moment to think about your clientele. Students are just kids. They can't always overcome, or even pretend to overcome, some of life's unpleasant blows. For example, in a group of fifty people, there may be a student who just failed a major test, another who was up all night because his or her parents were fighting, and yet another who is hungry with no money to pay for lunch. If your spouse suddenly filed for a divorce, or you just got word that your brother was in a serious accident, how interested in performing scales would you be? When students demonstrate a *pattern* of mis-behavior or lack of participation, then it's time to take action. On the other hand, some days students just have too many unrelated things on their minds to satisfy our plans without a little extra energy on our part. It's the nature of the business.

13

Good noise means learning. Bad noise means the children are out of control. No noise means adults don't understand the nature of children.

-Dr. Harlen Hansen
(University of Minnesota)-

What goes around comes around.

One thing you can be absolutely sure of is the fact that at least once in your teaching career, a student will test you. When all is said and done, however, let the matter rest. Students will make mistakes. Making poor choices and learning from them is a part of growing up. Be consistent in your discipline, but after the fact, for-give and forget. Put yourself in their shoes. If you were reprimanded by your principal and the situation was rectified, wouldn't you want the issue to be forgotten?

Yesterday is history. Tomorrow is a
mystery. Today is a gift...that's why
it's called the present.

Honor your students' opinions by never saying "you're wrong."

The combination of these words are crushing to
many students. In place of this, try something along
the lines of, "Help me to better understand your position," "I'm not sure I follow you," or better yet,
"Convince me." Similarly, if you sense that an incorrect
answer will cause a student to be ridiculed, you can
redirect the group's attention with a comment such as,
"I'm sorry, that's not the answer I am looking for...but
thanks for playing!" A sudden jolt of humor can provide
a wonderful diversion.

Freely admit when "you're wrong."

Accept it. You will inevitably make mistakes in
front of your students. And when you do, instead of
attempting to cover them up and appear free from
fault, make a point to voluntarily admit your errors. As
Dale Carnegie reminds us, "There's magic, positive
magic, in such phrases as: I may be wrong. I frequently am. And if I am wrong, I want to [make it] right."[12]
A sincere "My bad" or "Yes, I'm lost, let's try that
again" can go a long way in the never-ending quest to

14

build lasting, collaborative relationships. Your students will not think less of you. On the contrary, this reinforces the fact that you really are human, and honest mistakes are a natural part of growth.

Never be the one who ends "the hug."

Although the focus of this text is on the many things that music educators should give to their students, there is something that you should never give—Up! Students will always try your patience for both musical and non-musical reasons. However, giving up on a student is not a characteristic of an effective teacher, just as settling for "what you get" is not a characteristic of effective teaching. Begin on your students' level and then bring them to yours. If things don't go the way you had originally planned, try something else. Oftentimes a completely new approach or strategy is required. What really counts is being persistent in your quest for excellence and tenacious in your efforts to connect with each and every student.

Tulips bloom in the spring. Mums bloom in the fall.

If you were to ask yourself what constitutes a "loving parent," you would probably conclude that expressions of love involve providing basic human necessities (food, clothing, shelter), spending time together, unconditional acceptance and forgiveness, teaching independence, and random acts of kindness. It is also likely that building self-confidence would make the list. There are very few parents who would not want to see their children grow up to be secure, confident adults. Confidence is the key to a successful and happy life and is certainly an issue that loving parents are concerned with. In the realm of education, contributing to the development of a child's self-confidence is one of the most, if not the most, important expressions of love that a teacher can provide.

16

```
  I don't cause teachers trouble,
     My grades have been OK.
     I listen in my classes,
  And I'm in school every day.


   My teachers think I'm average.
    My parents think so too.
    I wish I didn't know that,
'Cause there's lots I'd like to do.


  I would like to build a rocket,
 I have a book that tells you how.
    Or start a stamp collection;
     Well, no use trying now.


 'Cause since I found I'm average,
   I'm just smart enough, you see,
   To know there's nothing special,
    That I should expect of me.
```

I'm part of that majority,
That hump part of the bell,
Who spends his life unnoticed,
In an average kind of hell.

-Anonymous-

Expect the best!

Your attitude has a profound effect on student behavior and performance. It can be said with absolute certainty that *you will get what you expect out of them.* If you anticipate that some of your students will do very well, that most will fall somewhere in the middle, and that a few will undoubtedly fail, this is likely to happen. On the other hand, if you act as though you expect all of your students to be motivated, hard working, and interested in music-making, then this is likely to happen as well. Set realistic expectations for students when you make practice assignments, conduct rehearsals, and hold discussions. The objective is to establish standards that are high enough to motivate students to do their best work, but not so high that students will inevitably be frustrated in trying to meet those expectations.[13] Although degrees of commitment and musicianship will undoubtedly vary from child to child, you must *believe(!)* that each and every student who "responds to your baton" possesses the innate capability to accomplish great things...including significant musical achievement.

> When I approach a child, he inspires
> me in two sentiments: tenderness for
> what he is, and respect for what he
> may become.
>
> -Louis Pasteur-

Search for the best in others.

18   One day the father of a very wealthy family took his son on a trip to the country for the firm purpose of showing him how less-fortunate people live. They spent a couple of days and nights on the farm of what would be considered a very poor family. On the return from their trip, the father said to his son, "Now do you understand what it's like to be poor?" "Oh, yeah," said the son. "And what did you learn from this trip?" asked the father. His son paused for a minute and then answered, "I saw that we have one dog and they have four. We have a pool that reaches to the middle of our garden and they have a creek that has no end. We have imported lanterns in our courtyard and they have the stars at night. We have a small piece of land to live on and they have fields that go beyond our sight. We have servants who serve us, and they serve others. We buy our food, and they grow theirs. We have walls around our property to protect us, and they have friends nearby to protect them." With this the boy's father was speechless. Then his son added, "Thanks Dad...for showing me how poor we are."

This story perfectly illustrates the concept of "perception is reality," which can have a profound influence on the ultimate success of your ensembles. Every student that you encounter will come bearing different gifts. Some will be capable of singing with heart-melting beauty, others will always sound like a "student." Some will be technical wizards, others will appear to be all thumbs. Some will dependable, some will be unpredictable. Some you would adopt as your own, while others raise the question, "Why did I ever decide to teach?" But most certainly, however, each and every one of your students will be good at something. Find that something, whether it is musical or not, and point it out! This builds self-confidence and creates a springboard for enhancing areas (musical and personal) that need improvement.

19

The greatest student musicians you will ever have the pleasure of teaching are those who believe in themselves.

Allow the ensemble to run through an easier section before diving into a difficult section.

By doing so, you are building confidence and mentally preparing them for more challenging tasks. Providing early opportunities for success also helps students to believe that achievement is possible.

End all rehearsals in a positive, fulfilling manner.

The last few minutes should be spent with everyone engaged in music making, not sitting there while you work with a section. This builds confidence by creating a sense of accomplishment.

Give your students ownership in the program.

Reach out and seek their thoughts, opinions, and ideas. The more you involve your students, the greater the tie-in with the program. All people feel more confident when they are able to contribute in meaningful ways. For example, kids have a way of relating to each other that eludes grown-ups, and it can be very helpful to allow your students to teach each other from time to time. This can be as simple as sending a couple of students into a practice room to work out a particularly troublesome passage. Another way to offer ownership is to allow students to contribute to the day-to-day operation of the program. You don't have to take the world upon your shoulders and do everything yourself. Establishing real positions with real responsibilities not only gives them an opportunity to contribute with purpose, but it also gives you more time to actually teach and deliver more of what students want most. Here are some possibilities:

President
• Conduct meetings and votes.

- Read the daily/weekly announcements.
- Hold group discussions.
- Send invitations to performances.
- Send Christmas and birthday cards.
- Send letters and thank-you notes.
- Organize and supervise special projects.
- Organize campaigns for recruiting new students.

Vice President(s)

- Organize social activities.
- Take pictures/videos of the group throughout the year.
- Maintain a group scrapbook.
- Organize after school workshops to help JH/MS students with their honor group audition music.

Secretary/Librarian(s)

- Maintain the music library.
- Help with general office work.
- Supervise alumni correspondence.

Rehearsal Manager (select a new student for this position on a regular basis)

- Take attendance.
- Post daily announcements.
- Prepare or set up any special items that are needed for rehearsal.
- Collect or pass out forms, assignments, written work, etc.
- Deliver messages to the office, other teachers, etc.

Stage Manager(s)

- Responsible for setting up chairs, stands, and any other special items for rehearsals and/or performances.

Equipment Manager(s)
- Make sure program logo is on all equipment.
- Organize and supervise loading crew.
- Make simple equipment repairs.
- Keep music stands tightened.

Loading Crew
- Responsible for loading, unloading, setting up, and tearing down all equipment.
- Give these students a specially-designed shirt, hat, pair of overalls, etc.
- Let these students eat first on trips.

Interior Decorator(s)
- Responsible for making sure things are always where they are supposed to be.
- Create, maintain, and update wall decorations, bulletin boards, etc.

Prepare for the unexpected.

Forty-five students and yourself are on a bus returning from district contest. The performance went very well and the group is deservedly excited. It is a fairly long bus ride and most students are visiting, a few are snacking, and others are catching up on their homework. As you peacefully recount the day's events, you are suddenly summoned by a frantic scream. You leap from your seat and head towards the back of the bus. Midway down the aisle, you freeze in your tracks. A few feet in front of you sits Tanner...who is purple...who is choking.

Although we would all like to believe that something like this would never happen to us, what if it did? What would you do? If your position could conceivably put you in such a situation, for example, you owe it to your students, their parents, and yourself to plan ahead. If you are not personally skilled in life-saving emergency procedures, by all means, keep someone around who is. When dealing with energetic, unpredictable adolescents, expecting the unexpected, particularly in terms of health and safety, is synonymous with concerned leadership.

23

Focus on your students' efforts, not on their abilities.

When students succeed, praise their efforts or their strategies, not their intelligence. Praising intelligence backfires by making students overly concerned with how smart they are and overly vulnerable to failure. In other words, help your students learn to value effort. Too many students think effort is only for the inept, yet sustained effort over time is the key to outstanding achievement.[14] It is the quest to reach new levels of performance excellence that ensures even greater performances in the future.

"You did it! Hard work and persistence will get you everywhere."

Focus on your students' strengths, not their weaknesses.

Research proves it time and time again. The most effective means of motivating student interest and effort is a learning environment conducive to risk taking and a teacher who overflows with encouragement. When in a rehearsal situation, resist the temptation to say the first thing that comes to your mind, which is usually negative:

"Basses, basses, basses, that's much too heavy! What are you guys thinking?"

Instead, try to address your point in a more positive manner:

"Basses, I appreciate the energy, but a lighter style is required in this section," or "We don't want to sound like elephants here, we want to sound like deer."[15]

Granted, this is much easier to say than it is to do "in the heat of the moment," but an affirmative approach will nonetheless be the greatest, and perhaps only, means of establishing a truly collaborative rehearsal atmosphere. The likelihood that students already know their weaknesses is good. Therefore, they don't need to be continuously reminded of them. What they do need is emphasis on their strengths and reassurance that they can achieve whatever they put their minds to. Besides, the typical reaction to criticism is to become defensive or withdrawn, which only serves to compound the problem that brought you to criticize them in the first place. The days of tyranny and intimidation are gone. Remove criticism and put-downs from your vocabulary and proceed down the roads of inspiration:

"You can do it!"
"What a great idea!"
"I know you can get it…just keep trying…you're almost there!"
"You're on the right track!"
"That's right!"
"Now you have it!"
"That's great!"
"Bravo!"
"Good for you!"
"Molto fantastico!"
"I knew you could do it!"
"I am very proud of you!"
"That's it!"
"Sensational!"
"Nice!"
"Well done!"

25

When dealing with young, impressionable minds and attitudes, *an encouraging course is the only path to follow.*

```
How high does the Sycamore grow? If you
cut it down, then you'll never know!

                          -Stephen Schwartz-
```

Dominant Themes: The Gift of Love

Making students feel welcome, important, and appreciated is vital to building long-term, productive relationships. For those who are committed to enriching lives through music, this is a constant priority.

In terms of conveying messages of love in the daily interactions between teachers and students, actions speak just as loud as words, and oftentimes more appropriately. Maintaining a calm yet firm presence in trying circumstances, for example, is not only the most effective means of restoring a controlled learning environment, but it also sends a silent yet clear, message of respect.

Never giving up on a student, or unconditional persistence, is one of the most important expressions of love that a teacher can impart. The pathway to success is not always straight and smooth; navigating this course requires a guide who is determined to see all passengers reach their destination...even if it means more than one trip.

People should be placed over prizes. Competition is healthy and in the best interest of both students and directors when it is used as a means to promote musical and personal growth. Competition is unhealthy, counterproductive, and even abusive when the program and/or the director's self-worth revolves solely around it. When music becomes more about winning and losing than enriching lives, everyone loses.

There is a direct correlation between achievement and self-confidence; students who believe in themselves are no strangers to success. Although there are many ways in which a teacher can contribute to the development of a child's self-confidence, positive expectations top the list. If a teacher expects his/her students to succeed, then this is likely to happen. If a teacher has low expectations for his/her students then this is likely to happen as well. Translated into words, high expectations say: "You are important to me. I believe in you. You are capable of accomplishing great things." This is a powerful expression of love.

28

the gift of
attention

All students long to be noticed. In fact, *100%
of 22,000 teachers* polled in a survey given by the
Carnegie Foundation described their students as
"emotionally needy and starved for attention and
affection."[16] This speaks for itself and emphasizes the
need to take (make!) the time to help each student feel
valued and important in positive ways. In *The Joy of
Inspired Teaching,* Dr. Tim Lautzenheiser illuminates
this point:

30

> We all want attention. Psychologists
> tell us it is the number one payoff for
> the human creature. Attention confirms
> our very existence. In many cases, it
> tells us we are needed. *The need to be needed*
> is one of the distinctions between man
> and other animals; in fact, for many
> it is more important than survival
> itself. Even those people who say they
> don't really want attention often say so
> because it gets them attention. Whether
> we receive approval or reprimand, we
> seek the acknowledgment of those around
> us and we guide our behavior according
> to the attention-rewards issued by those
> in our environment.[17]

For the vast majority of students, attention is like
chocolate—something they crave and never tire of. It
also serves as a means of compensation. Before

committing themselves for the long haul, the perception of pay-off must be great in the eyes of the student musician. "What's in this for me?" is a question that all students ask themselves, and it's up to you to supply them with satisfactory answers. Like the rest of us, students need to be frequently reminded that their *presence and efforts* are appreciated. Fortunately, it takes very little effort to satisfy this desire, and there are several painless yet powerful ways of giving your students "the time of day." **31**

Each day, the average child receives 12 minutes of attention from his or her parents. Unfortunately, there is no guarantee this attention is positive.

Focus on serving people, not the program.

Think of yourself as the CEO of a major public relations firm with your students as your clients. How much attention are your clients receiving? Could they be better served elsewhere? Invest your time and efforts in your students first, then take care of things like invoices, repairs, and copies. People behave according to how they feel, not what they know, and it is the wise director who seizes every opportunity to make a student feel special. A good rule of thumb is to

treat every student as you would want your own child
to be treated.

- As you make your way to school each day, in addition
to thinking about the usual grind (letters to write, orders
to place, music to prepare, etc.), give some thought to
the people you will encounter. Are there students who
seem to be down in the dumps lately? Is there something that you could do to give them a boost?

- When students are recognized for an accomplishment within the school or community, send them a
note (or e-mail) of congratulations. This shows that
you're thinking of them, and that you admire their
effort and achievement.

- Invite especially helpful students to your room for
lunch. Have a pizza delivered and tell them how
much you appreciate their hard work.

- Send a get-well message to a student who is fighting
an extended illness.

- Is one of your students in the hospital? Pay a visit.

- Has a student been absent for more than a couple of
days? A quick call or e-mail shows you noticed.

- Always say hello to your students when you see
them in the hall.

- Three-fourths of the people you will ever meet are
hungering and thirsting for sympathy. Give it to them,
and they will love you.[18]

"I don't blame you one bit for feeling that way. I would feel the same if I were you."

■ Is there a parent who needs a "wake-up call" about his or her child's behavior or progress?

 In a related vein, showing a little unexpected interest is an extremely powerful means of changing attitudes with difficult students.

The smallest good deed is better than the grandest intention.

33

Look at your students when they are talking to you.

This is such a basic thing, yet without even realizing it, many of us do not do it. We have become quite proficient at carrying on a conversation while doing multiple tasks. And if you're anything like me, there are even times in which you "pretend" to be listening when in reality you are thinking about something completely different than what the other person is talking about. If this is an issue that you need to work on, the solution is to slow down and remind yourself what's really important. The requisition, or whatever it is you are working on, will wait. When students speak to you, give them your undivided attention. Taking a moment to sincerely listen to what they have to say is the simplest way on earth of saying, "You are important to me."

Resist the urge to interrupt others or finish their sentences.

The practice of "pulling the words out from under someone" is another thing that most of us are guilty of from time to time. Yet as Richard Carlson reminds us, "If there's one thing almost everyone resents, it's someone who doesn't take the time to listen to what they are saying. And how can you really listen to what someone is saying when you are speaking for that person?"[19] The objective is to give attention, not take it. We're not talking about one of those magical moments where you finish someone else's sentence because you are so much alike or made for each other. This is just a conversation between you and a student. Yet by allowing the individual to speak without interruption, the interaction becomes a wonderfully simple way of affirming his or her value and importance.

34

Make it a goal to call at least one parent a week for the sole purpose of sharing something positive about their child.

It only takes a couple of minutes to pick up a phone and surprise a parent with some good news. The impact on the student's attitude, however, will last for days. Remember, *positive information to the home is unusual.*

Do your best to call on each and every student equally.

Vary whom you ask to provide musical models,

perform housekeeping tasks, answer questions, etc.

Acknowledge courage, respect, self-control, effort, and honor whenever possible.

Whatever gets attention gets repeated! Jump on every opportunity to publicly recognize these qualities.

Do not acknowledge negative comments or actions.

Whatever gets attention gets repeated! The students who are given the greatest amount of your attention will literally determine the dominant attitude of the group.[20] When students act up, instead of recognizing the adverse behavior, pick up the momentum of the rehearsal and redirect the attention of the group away from these students. The best time to deal with negative attitudes or actions is after class in a private setting. By handling the situation in this way, you will preserve the integrity of the rehearsal, you will hold students accountable for their actions, and *you will choose to lead and not be lead.*

35

When we choose to criticize in private and praise in public, we are opting to water the flowers while hoeing the weeds— a guaranteed technique for a superior musical garden.[21]

-Dr. Tim Lautzenheiser-

When the same student acts up day after day, remind yourself that he/she is desperately seeking attention.

As difficult as it may be sometimes, the most effective way of "calming" certain students is to give them the extra attention they crave. This refers to those who come close but never really cross the line. They do little things that don't really warrant "discipline," yet they're still a frequent source of stress and interruption in the rehearsal. For example, I once had a student who was a very talented young musician, but could not sit still long enough to even begin to mold his potential. If there were a way of doing something different, he would be doing it. If there were a sudden eruption on the left side of the room, he would be the cause of it. To make matters worse, whenever I addressed his shenanigans, it just seemed to provide fuel for him to continue. After a few days of frustration, it finally dawned on me that what this student really wanted was not trouble, but attention. So, to satisfy this need without intruding on the rehearsal or taking time away from other students, I pulled him aside after rehearsal and told him that for the next few days I wanted him to be the first one in the room and that when he arrived to immediately come and see me. The very next day he was the first to show up and he found me sitting on the podium patiently waiting to greet him. For the first couple of days he would say something like, "Well, I'm here. What do you want?" Of course I expected such and didn't answer. Instead, I asked him to have a seat next to me and then started a conversation directed at all the good things that occurred on the day before. My thinking was that if I acknowledged all the positive things he had done (which was a task in itself at the beginning) and completely ignored the negative things, perhaps he would try harder to do more of the things that I was praising him for. Much to my surprise, it worked. In fact, it worked so well that even as our brief conversations faded, his behavior continued to improve and before long he became a model student. To this day, I am still amazed at how such little effort on my part had such a profound effect. It took only a couple of minutes to satisfy this student's desperate need for attention, but the impact lasted throughout the entire course of the year. It just goes to show how giving in inches can move you forward in miles.

37

Additional ideas for giving extra (positive!) attention to students who need it.

Comments:
" I really like the way Adam is articulating the notes in this phrase."

"Aaron, I appreciate your patience today."

Tasks:
"Bryce, please run this note to the office for me."

"Bryan, please run the tape deck for us today."

"Alisha, please demonstrate how measure 12 should be played."

"Tori, please play that phrase again. You did such a great job, and I just want to hear it one more time."

Make sure each student's name is visible somewhere in the room.

This is a form of *silent attention* that really makes students feel like they belong. Lockers, bulletin boards, and individual mailboxes are all great candidates for this.

Make sure all of your students receive special recognition every now and then.

■ Send "sunshine grams" or "gotcha awards" as a little boost of encouragement for anything that you feel is worth recognizing.

■ Mail each of your students a birthday card. This may seem like a lot of work, particularly if you have large ensembles, but going this extra mile is more than worth it. Imagine what a surprise this would be for a student who didn't even think you knew his/her name. This simple act instantly invokes the thought, "Wow, he noticed me," and is a very effective way of acknowledging your students' value. The sad truth is that your card may very well be the only card that some students receive.

 This could also be the factor that sways a student who is "on the bubble" to remain in the program.

■ If you see that one of your students is in the newspaper, cut the article/picture out, have it laminated, and then mail it to the student with a note of congratulations.

■ Give Hugs™ or Kisses™ candies to deserving students for everyday successes.

■ Recognize/reward the "Play of the Day."

■ Recognize/reward the "Section of the Week."

■ Create a "Hall of Fame" for students who go above and beyond to help or represent the program.

39

> The job of the conductor is to manipulate creatively the events so there is always something to reward.
>
> -Frederick Fennell-

Image is (almost) everything.

Peer acceptance and approval is an issue that can have a tremendous impact on your program. As George Hopkins, Director of the Cadets of Bergen County, puts it, "What students want more than anything is to *look good.*" If the student body perceives your program negatively, it will be difficult, if not impossible, to attract and keep students. It is imperative to protect the image of those who have committed their time and energy to music.

■ Do not ask your students to wear used, outdated uniforms. If finances do not allow for immediate purchase of new uniforms, get together with a few crafty parents and/or students and come up with a suitable alternative.

■ Highlight individual and group accomplishments in the school announcements.

40

■ When performing at school assemblies, choose music that the student body will enjoy. It is also vital for this music to be performed well. If you're not sure what to pick, ask your students. They'll know!

■ Purchase a set of classy music folders to use during performances only.

■ Establish a program logo. Encourage individual sections to create their own.

■ Make it possible for students to earn a school letter with subsequent bars.

■ Include students in the design and selection process of group t-shirts, jackets, etc.

At the end of the year, give each of your students an award or keepsake.

Examples of traditional awards

- Exceptional Musician
- Performer Of The Year
- Most Improved
- Above And Beyond
- Outstanding Freshman/Sophomore/Junior/Senior
- Esprit De Corps

Examples of humorous awards
- Most Blunt And Unpredictable
- Most Vocally Expressive
- Top Squeaker
- Most Grooviest
- Most Likely To Become A Band/Orchestra/Choir Director
- Most Likely To Play Their Instrument Or Sing For Friends At The Bus Stop

41

 These award ideas came directly from students. The collective creativity of a typical band, orchestra, or choir is amazing. If given the chance, your groups will come up with some very clever and crazy ideas as well.

Keepsake ideas:
- *Have a custom CD made.* This is a great keepsake item that doubles as a fundraiser. Make this project easier on yourself by recruiting a few parents to take care of recording your group's performances. This also gives you a broad base of music to choose from when compiling songs for the CD.

- *Music note key chain or pin*
    8th note for freshman
    16th note for sophomores
    32nd note for juniors
    64th note for seniors

- *Pen/pencil embossed with the program logo*

- *Certificate of participation with a quote or saying that is reflective of the year. For example:*

"Pride is a personal commitment. It is an attitude which separates excellence from mediocrity. It is that ingredient which inspires us not to get ahead of others, but rather to get ahead of ourselves."[22]

42

In addition to direct efforts on your part, it is important to **be pro-active in seeking attention and support for your students from others.** *To accomplish this, keep the "circle of giving" fresh in your mind, as giving always leads to receiving.*

Give to your fellow teachers.
- Provide information on events/students that will affect their classes.

- Make sure you are open to giving some of your class time if you expect to take some of theirs.

- Periodically leave snacks in the lounge with a note saying, "Thanks for all you do to support our program."

- Have your students deliver a small potted plant to each teacher with a note saying, "Thanks for helping our program grow."

- Leave an invitation to a special performance in their school mailbox.

Give to your administration.

- Recognize all principals, administrators, and school-board members at concerts and publicly thank them for their support.

- Give them complimentary items that promote your program (i.e. t-shirts, hats, pens).

- Keep them informed about what's happening in your program through the use of e-mails, newsletters, or FYI notes in their school mailboxes.

- Give them fair warning when trouble is brewing.

- Send them an invitation to a special performance.

- Give them an annual report on the program.[23]

43

Give to your school-support staff.

- Surprise them with some homemade goodies.

- Give them a Christmas gift.

- Send them a note of appreciation.

- Give them complimentary fundraising items.

- Send them an invitation to a special performance.

Give to your parents.

It's no secret. Thriving music programs almost always have a tremendous amount of parental involvement. Here are a few key suggestions for keeping this vital line of support active and eager to help:

■ Communicate early and often with parents. Make it a priority to frequently share news about what and how their children are doing through newsletters, phone calls, and e-mails (possibly even with digital pictures).

■ Schedule short parent meetings in conjunction with concerts that focus on ways they can encourage their children, help with practice, care for instruments/voices, etc. Parents need to know that they are not alone, and that all children have "musical hurdles" to get over from time to time. Let them know they have made a wise investment and always reinforce the values of formal musical training.

■ Provide parents with plenty of opportunities to get involved. Stress the fact that their involvement enables them to be an active part of their children's lives outside the home. Children grow up so fast and opportunities such as this are few and far between. A volunteer form, such as the one on page 45, is a good way to get things rolling.

■ Instead of having "booster meetings," have "parent nights," and make sure they last no longer than one hour. Parents should not be required to have stamina to make it through a meeting. Here is an example of an agenda that will keep them coming back:
• Have minutes of last meeting, treasurer's reports, meeting agenda, and program update available upon arrival. Live background music by student performers is also nice.
• Start the meeting on time.

Student's Name: Grade:

Mother

Name   home mailing address

home phone   work phone

May we contact you   Email address
briefly at work?

Father

Name   home mailing address

home phone   work phone

May we contact you   Email address
briefly at work?

Please share any special information about your child that will help us to better meet his/her needs. This information will be kept confidential.

Please indicate if either or both parents can help in any of the following areas (M=Mother, F=Father):

Fund raising	M___ F___		Carpentry	M___ F___
Public Relations	M___ F___		Welding	M___ F___
First Aid	M___ F___		Photography	M___ F___
Uniforms	M___ F___		Baking	M___ F___
Equipment Moving	M___ F___		Sewing	M___ F___
Office Help	M___ F___		Telephone Calling	M___ F___
Notary Public	M___ F___		Merchandising/Souvenirs	M___ F___
Truck/Trailer Driving	M___ F___		Printing	M___ F___
Trip Sponsor	M___ F___		Graphic Design/Layout	M___ F___
Video Taping	M___ F___		Party/Banquet Planning	M___ F___
Piano Accompaniment	M___ F___			

Please indicate if you have any contacts with people in the following businesses:

Costumes	M___ F___		Lodging	M___ F___
Dance wear	M___ F___		Printing	M___ F___
Athletic wear	M___ F___		Restaurants	M___ F___
Fabric sales	M___ F___		Transportation	M___ F___
Graphic designs	M___ F___		Trophies/Awards	M___ F___

Please list any special skills that you would be willing to share.

- Begin with a warm welcome by the president of the organization.
- Discuss major events such as fundraisers, trips, upcoming performances, etc.
- Schedule special reports and guest speakers.
- Feature director reports and comments from student leaders.
- Stage live student performances or videos of student performances.
- Provide refreshments and time for visitation.

■ At the end of each year, give each booster club member a token of your appreciation.
Examples:

- CD of the group's performances
- Coffee mugs with the group's logo
- Calendar
- Small basket filled with Hugs™ and Kisses™ candy
- Special coupon books (have these made if you use a coupon-book fundraiser)

Any of these items could be hand delivered by a small group of students to add a personal touch.

■ Establish a web site for your program. This is a great way to provide your parents with information. Here are just a few of the things that could be included:

- performance calendars and announcements
- rehearsal schedules date and/or time changes
- trip information
- access to student account information (with a password)
- sign-ups for program-related events general information about the program
- email links to directors and staff members
- links to other school and music-related web sites

- audio/visual bytes of student performances
- Order forms for program-related items

■ Give your parents insight into the many values of participating in school music ensembles. Stress the fact that formal music study can increase the quality of their child's life and that those who teach it are handing present and future generations a gift with values that we are only beginning to be understand. The following are some examples that can have a tremendous impact. Include at least one quote similar to these in every piece of correspondence that you send to parents...and see that your administrators receive a copy as well.

47

> Music education is not merely desirable, but essential, to the full development of every student. The primary values of MUSIC and music education overlap the essential life values that most individuals and societies pursue for the good of each and all: personal growth, differentiation, complexity, enjoyment, self-esteem, and happiness. The welfare of a society depends on the ability of its citizens to pursue and achieve these values regularly. The quality of individual and community depends on providing people with the knowings and the opportunities they require to make a life as well as a living. [24]
>
> -David Elliot-

Musicians surpass the finest athletes in motor performance, complexity, and precision.

>   -George P. Moore- (*Professor of Biomedical Engineering, University of Southern California*)

The arts not only enhance the quality of our lives; they help us to think in creative ways. Education without the arts is like a building with no windows. Learning takes place there, but without the same vision and perspective.

48

>   -Jane Jayroe- *(Former Miss America)*

General Electric hires a lot of engineers. We want young people who can do more than add up a string of numbers and write a coherent sentence. They must be able to solve problems, communicate ideas, and be sensitive to the world around them. Participation in the arts is one of the best ways to develop these abilities.

>   -Clifford V. Smith-
>   *(President of the General Electric Foundation)*

Music is a primary condition of the human experience. In the history of man on earth, many civilizations have been identified that could not read, write, or calculate. None have been discovered that did not make music.[25]

-Eugene Corporon-

The essence of school-music ensembles is cooperative learning, which offers many important advantages:
- Cooperative learning helps students to develop the skills of leadership, communication, decision making, and conflict management they need for future success in school and in a career.

49

- Cooperative learning develops interdependence. The success of the group is dependent on the achievement of each member, and students become committed to helping each other to succeed.

- Cooperative learning contributes to the development of self-esteem because it promotes positive peer relationships and better social skills.

- In cooperative learning settings, students realize that their ideas can be useful to others. This boosts self-confidence.[26]

In March of 2000, members of Congress submitted a resolution expressing, "The sense of Congress regarding the benefits of music education." The resolution moves that, "Music education enhances intellectual development and enriches that academic environment for all ages" and "Music educators greatly contribute to the artistic, intellectual, and social development of American children, and play a key role in helping children to succeed in school."[27]

There is a direct correlation between improved SAT scores and the length of time spent studying the arts. Those who studied the arts four or more years scored 59 points higher on verbal and 44 points higher on math portions of the SAT than students with no course-work or experience in the arts.[28]

"While the typical classroom is doing lower level learning ninety percent of the time (knowledge, com-prehension, application), school-music ensembles are already at advanced levels of learning at the down-beat. We are constantly analyzing and we are constantly synthesizing. The evaluation process is never-ending."[29]

Give to your community.

- Hold a "pops" concert at a local park (with free popcorn!).
- Give a holiday concert at a local mall.
- Perform at meetings of local clubs and civic organizations.
- Hold a free car wash.
- Perform at local retirement and nursing homes.
- Perform or volunteer at annual town events.
- Send patrons a handwritten thank-you note for their support of a fundraiser.
- Make arrangements for a special performance to be aired on a local cable channel.
- Recruit students to volunteer at the Special Olympics.
- Highlight group accomplishments and keep a steady supply of information about the program in the local newspaper.
- Recruit students to assist with local charities and service organizations.
- Recruit students to help with Salvation Army bell ringing during the holidays.

- *When you find a fundraiser that's not broken, don't fix it.* The Girl Scouts didn't start baking cookies overnight. The monumental success of this fundraiser evolved over the course of several years. Thus, when you find something that seems to go over well, stick with it. Not only will this be more profitable in the long run, it says to your community that the program is stable and worthy of support. "I wonder what they'll sell this year" is not something you want to hear. Give your community a quality product or service to look forward to *at the same time each year,* and the support will come. It is also a good idea to limit the number of fundraisers used that involves direct sales to the community. In most towns, there are many organizations competing for the same financial support, and you don't want to connect your program with groups that are constantly hitting patrons with another "thing to buy." At a loss for ideas? Here are a few possibilities for starters:

  - ✎ Sell concessions at sporting events.
  - ✎ Host a contest or festival.
  - ✎ Start a recycling business.
  - ✎ Consider using gift certificates:

51

Gift Certificate

To _____

From _____

A contribution of _____ has been
credited to your music account.

Happy Holidays!

Dominant Themes: The Gift of Attention

For virtually all students, few things rank higher
in importance than positive acknowledgment from
others. Steady doses of affirmation satisfy the need to
be needed and motivate the recipient to receive more
of the same. In the context of student-teacher relationships, this equals increased effort and a willingness to
work together.

One way or another, students will find a way to get **53**
the attention they need. If positive attention is not
readily available, negative attention will often suffice.

From monumental achievements to modest acts of
improvement, opportunities for awarding positive
attention can be found around every corner.

There are as many ways to give attention as there are
reasons to give it. From elaborate acts of recognition to
a single, kind word, the instruments of acknowledgment
come in all shapes and sizes.

A teacher's efforts to give his/her students positive
attention can be multiplied many times over by recruiting the assistance of others. Education is a partnership
between teachers, support personnel, administrators,
and the community at large. Each group plays an
important role in a school family and can provide
students with unique forms of attention. Gaining this

attention from any or all of these groups requires nothing less than giving the same. Start with the basics, such as communication (keeping others informed on past, present, and future events) and gratitude (showing appreciation for the efforts of others). Once this is accomplished, you can proceed to give even more by incorporating or expanding upon any of the ideas presented in this section. Those who walk the pathway of giving walk a two-way street. Nurture a small seed, yield a bountiful crop.

the gift of accomplishment

As professional educators, our prime directive is to do everything possible to help all students achieve and succeed; in other words, to **engineer student success.** This holds especially true for those who are reluctant to learn. Despite the way it may appear sometimes, no one really wants to struggle, earn last chair, or be thought of as a "clueless wonder." The desire for knowledge and growth is innate in all students, as is the potential for significant musical achievement.

Success breeds success.

Operate within an *Instructional Framework* that enables all students to succeed.

It should come as no surprise that in order for all students to become skilled music-makers, an instructional plan that caters to individual learners must be utilized. There are many ways to accomplish this. In fact, every director, professor, book, etc. you consult on the subject will likely offer varying strategies. Furthermore, each combination of director, students, school, and program will require a somewhat different approach. Thus, the following discussion on organizing, implementing, and assessing instruction is presented specifically as a resource of options. These ideas are targeted at creating an *instructional framework* that caters to each individual student as well as the group. After all, how would you feel if your child got "lost in the shuffle" and missed out on the many substantial values that formal music training has to offer?

The musician in all of us longs to be heard.

Foundations
There are several important factors that serve as foundations for creating a framework for effective musical teaching and learning.

57

■ *It is vital that students master key music fundamentals.*
There are "common ground" skills and concepts (aural, translative, and dexterous) that are applicable to the performance of most musical works. Such fundamentals must be thoroughly taught/learned, as well as continuously reinforced.

■ *There must be a proper balance between fundamentals and application.*
All work and no play is a formal invitation for students to leave the program. Each year of participation should bring new and exciting music-making challenges. Fun-seeking teenagers quickly lose interest in the "same stuff...different day, week, month, or year" approach.

■ *Music education is riveted with opportunities to teach things that are not musical.*
The nature and scope of this profession puts music directors in the unique position to teach things such as

self-discipline, commitment, teamwork and responsibility; all of which are substantial human values in and of themselves. In fact, it could be argued that this is just as essential, if not more, than teaching music. Who could dispute the importance of learning to be punctual, following procedures, working with diverse others, and meeting deadlines? Without question, music education is not only about teaching music, it's an undertaking that requires nurturing basic life skills and attributes as well. And as Mark Scharenbroich advocates, we should seize every opportunity to teach more than just subject matter, *not because we have to, but because we can.*[30]

> Since music has so much to do with the molding of character, it is necessary that we teach it to our children.
>
> -Aristotle-

■ *It is important to keep the program as a whole in perspective.* If allowed to do so, this profession will consume your life. Music directors need a system of planning, implementing, and assessing instruction that is manageable, uncomplicated, and efficient. When in school, the majority of your time should be spent with students, not paperwork; when out of school, the majority of your time should be spent doing what you want, not school work. Make it a priority to take time for non-musical things, such as reading, travel, spending time with family and friends, etc. Not only is this good for your mental well-being, but it also enables you to give more to your students. As Tim Lautzenheiser reminds us, the more experiences you have to parallel the music you are working on, the more stories you can tell, the better you can stimulate your students' imaginations.[31]

 In a related vein, a considerable percentage of students will be involved in multiple activities, and if the program is overly time consuming, many will choose not to continue.

■ *The teaching/learning process in school must motivate students to practice out of school.*

Music programs must be practice friendly. No matter how great the curriculum, or how effective your teaching is, without consistent practice, students will not realize their potential. Motivation to practice must be a high priority. Directly and indirectly, it has to be meticulously woven into all dimensions of instruction.

59

■ *Performance progress must be assessed on a regular basis; otherwise, students will not practice.*

As much as we would like to think that our teaching provides all the motivation students need to practice on their own, the fact of the matter is that accountability is the real driving force. The key here is to make this procedure as painless and efficient as possible.

■ *The method book is a powerful instructional tool, but not a curriculum.*

Amidst the hustle and bustle of a typical school year, it is so easy to allow method books to assume roles they are not designed to play. For example, a prominent goal for any musician is to develop the ability to consistently produce a full, beautiful tone. The method book of your choosing may have great exercises to address this, but the real objective is tone production, not performing line four on page five. Fundamental musicianship evolves by encouraging students to conquer a continuous stream of progressive developmental activities that are targeted at specific skills and concepts, not just an occasional tone study or "rhythmic chant." Meaningful application of these fundamentals comes from engaging in a variety of compelling music-making challenges, not just a two-line unison version of Beethoven's 9th.

> Teachers who have no curriculum follow the [method book] page by page, cover to cover, and look for busywork for the students. When this happens, you have students who walk into the classroom and say things like this:
>
> "Are we going to do anything today?" "Are we going to do anything important today?" "Did I miss anything important while I was absent?"[32]
>
> -Harry K. Wong-

At the other end of the spectrum, there are many significant advantages to using a quality series of method books **(MBs):**
- MBs offer a variety of material for the development of basic music fundamentals, particularly the teaching of musical notation.
- MBs often include songs in a variety of musical styles.
- MBs can be used as a resource for home-practice material.
- Major breaks in the MBs can be used to delineate units, particularly in the first few years of instruction.

- MBs often contain great illustrations of proper posture, playing positions, etc.
- MBs often contain important instrument/voice-care instructions.

When part of a well-balanced program of instruction, method books can be a powerful tool for nurturing young musicians. Strategic use must prevail, however. You don't want students to exit your classes answering the question, "What did you learn in music this year?" with, "Book one!"

■ *Whether working with one student or a hundred, fundamental principles of teaching and learning must be incorporated into the overall instructional process.*[33]

61

- *All learners do not learn at the same rate. They should be given opportunities to move at their own pace. This is especially true when developing technical ability.*

- *All learners do not learn in the same style. Learning must be in small steps that integrate into a meaningful whole.*

- *Assignments must be structured and clear.*

- *Learning is increased when objectives/goals are easily recognized and attainable.*

- *Mastering complex neuromuscular tasks often requires much repetition. Instruction should include both guided and independent practice.*

- *Class time must be used efficiently with minimum time spent on non-instructional activities.*

- *Certain concepts and/or skills are best learned in individual or small group settings.*

- *The best teaching is that which encourages students to think for themselves and develop their own evaluative process.*

- *Cooperative learning leads to higher achievement for all students.*

■ *Student attention and interest determines the degree of productivity in rehearsals.*

Regardless of your great conducting abilities or grand intentions, if students are unfocused or uninterested, little will be accomplished.

62

As overwhelming as this may seem, it is quite possible to accommodate all of these foundational elements within your teaching. Furthermore, the entire process can be both student and teacher friendly. This task requires and revolves around the following:

I. Class work based on three inter-dependent components

II. A realistic plan for encouraging independent study

III. The Mastery Learning Model (ML)

The combination of these elements creates a versatile framework for organizing, implementing, and assessing a progressive series of meaningful learning experiences; in other words, *an infrastructure for comprehensive musical instruction.*

Part I: Class Work

For instructional and organizational clarity, *Class Work* is divided into three inter-dependent components. Each component is necessary and dependent on the others for success; each component affects and is affected by the others.

A. Conduct and Participation

The primary objective of this component is to establish a setting that is conducive to effective teaching and learning. Most directors have more than enough musical expertise to provide their students with meaningful music-making experiences. This knowledge is useless, however, unless it is presented to a receiving mind.

63

Artistic musical performances require a mental and physical state of relaxed concentration. Ultra rigid environments are tense environments, and as every seasoned musician knows, tension is a performer's worst enemy. On the other hand, when students have too much freedom, there will always be those who take advantage of the situation by not participating, moving around the room without permission, or saying whatever they want whenever they want. It can be said with absolute certainty that if personal responsibilities and rehearsal procedures are not taught, learned, and fulfilled with consistency, there will be many struggles in the day-to-day operation of the program, as well as mediocre musical outcomes. The solution is to **create an environment that lies at the intersection of comfort and control.**

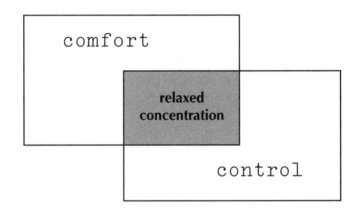

Control
✔ Students look at the conductor when he/she is addressing the group.
✔ Students stop immediately when the conductor gives a cut-off.
✔ Students keep an eye on the conductor at all times.
✔ Students remain in their assigned positions (seats) unless given permission to move.
✔ Students are ready to begin rehearsals on time, and with all necessary materials.
✔ Students raise their hands and wait to be called on when they have a question.
✔ Students know when it is appropriate to visit and when it is not.

Comfort

✔ Students are not afraid to take musical risks.

✔ Students are not afraid to make honest mistakes.

✔ Students are not afraid to ask for help when needed.

✔ Students believe that the director will not put them on the spot or embarrass them.

Achieving a classroom environment that promotes relaxed concentration involves many things. It is a reflection of both the teacher's ability to read, relate, and respond to students, as well as the overall struc- **65** ture and content of the class. If you think for a minute that students will automatically give you their undivided attention just because "it's the right thing to do," think again. You (the conductor, motivator, peacemaker, etc.) have to capture their attention at each and every meeting. Indeed, a single, magic answer for establishing comfort and control just does not exist. There are, however, steps which can be taken that will certainly help.

 As you read through the following list, keep in mind that the greatest means of maintaining a comfortable, controlled learning environment is to keep students actively engaged in purposeful, interesting learning activities.

■ Establish, monitor, and enforce classroom procedures and behavioral expectations. (*See Teach your students to C.A.R.E., page* 156)

■ Reinforce proper fulfillment of rehearsal procedures

and behavioral expectations by giving frequent praise and awarding daily conduct and participation points.

■ *Throughout the process of preparing for the first performance, make it your ultimate goal (above all other issues!) to teach your students how to rehearse like a great band/orchestra/choir.* Stress the fact that this is the key to success for the remainder of the year.

■ Prominently post your agenda and objectives for each and every rehearsal in a consistent location. Be clear about what is going to happen, and insist that students get all required materials in order before rehearsal. This cuts down on "transition" time (a.k.a. disruption time) and helps build teamwork. Students are more engaged in the rehearsal when they see purpose and direction in their efforts.

■ Get the school year off to a great start. It is vital to begin the year with the message that you are confident, competent, and in control. Have an assigned seat ready for each student when he/she arrives. This establishes immediate authority, and makes the dreaded task of taking roll so much easier. It is also a good idea to have a short project waiting for them in their seats as well. This could be a questionnaire, an info form, a musical puzzle, etc. Once students are seated, begin the business of the class immediately. It is essential to know exactly what you expect to accomplish and precisely how you expect to accomplish it. Reassure students that they can do well in your course, and explain exactly what they must do in order to succeed. Make it a goal to have students leave your class on the first day feeling like they have learned something, and most of all, wanting to come back for more.

■ Engage your students in meaningful activity as soon as possible. Make it your first priority in every rehearsal to get students on task, *not* to take roll, fix horns, fill out grade checks, listen to excuses, etc. The prime time for learning is the first few minutes of rehearsal, and it is essential to take care of **housekeeping tasks** without the group sitting idle or interrupting the flow of the rehearsal. The importance of this cannot be over emphasized.

Ideas For Taking Roll   **67**

• Make an attendance board that holds key chains (or key tags on fishing line swivels) labeled with each student's name. As students enter the room, they simply go to the board and turn their key chain over. Check the board for any names that are still showing and mark these students absent.

• Place a pencil (wrapped with a computer label with the student's name on it) in a special container (e.g. a coffee can or shoe box) for each section of an ensemble. Teach students to pick up their pencil as they enter the room and begin preparing for rehearsal. Check the containers for remaining pencils and mark these students absent. A great bonus to this idea is that your students always have a pencil to use during rehearsal. Obviously, you must also teach students that part of the closing procedures for rehearsal includes putting their pencils back in the right containers.

• Label each student's music folder with his/her name.

When the students come in, they are to take their folders and begin preparing for rehearsal. Check for any remaining folders and mark these students absent.

- *Train* an exceptionally-conscientious student to take roll.

- Try taking roll at the end of rehearsal by having your students return to their seats after they have put everything up for the day. This procedure eliminates the need for corrections to your attendance records due to late arrivals and also gives the group a little "bonding" time. Keep in mind that you must be disciplined enough to stop rehearsal in time to get attendance tasks completed. If you begin rehearsals immediately, however, this system can be quite effective.

68

Ideas For Making Announcements

- Reduce announcement time by obtaining a calendar or dry erase board that is as large as you can possibly accommodate. Hang this in a prime location and use it for posting all events, deadlines, etc. Give your students the responsibility of always knowing what's on this calendar. You could even test them on it every now and then.

- Teach students that questions are not to be asked when you are giving announcements. Explain that the appropriate time to ask questions is when you ask for questions. Experience has shown that when student questions are intermittently mixed within announcements, it often turns into a "visit fest." Besides, chances are good that most questions will be answered anyway when you are allowed to complete your announcements without interruption.

You could also make it standard procedure for students to ask questions on an individual basis *after* rehearsal.

- Give announcements/instructions one time and one time only. If you repeat yourself, students will not listen the first time.

- If a student repeatedly has trouble paying attention when you are making announcements, assign him/her the task of writing the announcements down as you give them.

Organizational Ideas

69

- Install student mailboxes (like those found in teacher lounges). In addition to making students feel important, mailboxes are great organizational and communication tools.

- Post goals and important notices in highly visible locations...such as next to the clock!

- Create an "in-box" for collecting the things that students will need to turn in throughout the year. Stress that everything must have a "return address" (a.k.a. the student's name). You may find it helpful to create one of these for each class.

■ Consider including "conductor-less" warm-ups:

In a band rehearsal, the first measure of each exercise could be performed by a percussionist. In an orchestra rehearsal, the first measure could be performed by a first-chair player on the first pitch of the exercise. In a choir rehearsal, the first measure could be performed by a student pianist on the first pitch of the exercise.

Incorporating this type of warm-up exercise in the first few minutes of rehearsal gives you a window of time to take roll, deal with students needing extra attention, and make sure that everyone is on task. After just a few days of this it will become routine, and you can proceed with the business of the rehearsal in as little as two or three minutes. Students "get with it" much quicker when they know you will be moving around the room and monitoring their actions.

■ Begin rehearsals by using a hand signal, which indicates that each performer is to play or sing a certain pitch (e.g. holding up one finger). Once all eyes are upon you, give them a cut-off and immediately proceed with a warm-up exercise that requires students to watch the conductor (e.g. "molto rubato" long tones). This helps establish eye contact and mental focus from the very beginning. Of course, it's up to you to maintain this focus throughout the remainder of the rehearsal (i.e. minimal down time, meaningful music-making projects, the absence of mindless repetition, etc.).

■ Be ready! Set an example of preparedness for your students.

✔ Chairs and music stands are in order.
✔ New music is passed out.
✔ Instrument/equipment storage units are open.
✔ Recording equipment is set up and turned on.
✔ CDs to be played are cued and ready.
✔ Special collection boxes are in clear view.
✔ Scores are in order.
✔ Rehearsal plans are posted.

■ When engaged in a rehearsal situation that requires frequent starts and stops, tell the students exactly where to begin and where to end. For example: "Please start at measure twelve and stop when you get to twenty-four." This is an effective means of avoiding situations in which students continue to play or sing for several seconds after you indicate a cut-off. During the initial use of this strategy, stress that their ability to follow instructions is of much greater concern to you than anything musical.

■ When speaking to the whole class, make sure the first words out of your mouth are positive and directed at giving your students something to look forward to. This is a form of "anticipatory set." Here are a few examples:

• Share the goals for the rehearsal.
• Praise yesterday's rehearsal and encourage them to surpass it (*"You performed _____ so well yesterday. I can hardly wait to hear what happens today."*)
• Remind them of an upcoming performance and the need to get a lot accomplished. Stress how impressed

their family and friends will be at the next performance.

- *"Today I'm going to challenge you by _____ ."*

- *"Today we are going to see if you can perform _____ up to a tempo that will really make the piece exciting."*

- *"By the end of today's rehearsal you will know how to _____."*

■ Speak with intensity, not volume. A soft tone of voice invites students to listen more attentively. An added benefit of this is that when you do have to raise your voice, you will really have their attention.

72

■ Insist that students raise their hands and wait to be called on when they would like to ask a question or provide an answer.

 ■ What students don't learn is more important than what they do learn. Teach them that:

- You are not just a "threatening/repeating" teacher.
- It is not okay to say whatever you want whenever you want.
- Daily participation is not optional; it is mandatory.
- It is not acceptable to ignore rehearsal procedures after the first two weeks of school.

■ Give *closure* to your rehearsals.

- Praise good things that happened in the rehearsal.
- Encourage improvement in areas that still require work.
- Acknowledge individual students for special musical and/or non-musical achievements.
- Give reminders: practice assignments, special class events, special school events, where things go

(music, cases), etc.

- Ask students who need attention (for positive and/or negative reasons) to see you immediately.
- Dismiss students with a genuinely felt "Have a good day!"

■ Make a "great rehearsal jar" and fill it with marbles. Take a marble out after each great rehearsal and put a marble back in for not-so-great rehearsals. When the jar is empty, throw a party. Another option is to use *tallies.* Put a mark in a prominent location after every great rehearsal. Erase a mark after every not-so-great rehearsal. Once the group earns x-number of marks, reward them for it. These strategies work best with grade school and middle school students.

73

■ Let students know that you really are a normal person (and that they are in good hands) by creating a display case containing pictures from your childhood and artifacts such as old books, awards, and trophies. You could also include diplomas, favorite books, hobbies, souvenirs from places you have traveled or toured, memorabilia from college, special plaques/certificates, pictures of your family, etc. Including a personal bio in a concert program or the course syllabus also helps with this.

■ Stress the importance of teamwork. In group endeavors, nothing works without teamwork. It is the glue that holds everything together, and requires a two-sided commitment from each member. First, is the musical side. The ensemble as a whole depends on each musician to master his or her individual part. Everyone is a starter, an important link in the musical chain. A chain, however, is only as strong as the weakest link, which means that everyone must give their very best effort towards accomplishing established musical goals. Eugene Corporon provides us with a great analogy regarding this:

> ...think of the rehearsal as a musical-assembly plant. The music gets put together at the plant. It is assembled each day and we listen to it work, all the while noticing what still needs to be improved. At the end of the rehearsal, we disassemble the artwork and send a part of it home with every musician. Each agrees to work on their part so that it will fit better next time the piece is reassembled. Obviously, when a part is missing or not being played well, the composition is less than whole and progress is impended. In a very real sense, all musicians have the opportunity to bring a gift to rehearsal, something they make themselves at home...a beautiful part.[34]

The other side of this commitment involves the non-musical things that must be given by and shared between each member of the group:

Compassion: showing understanding and appreciation towards the work and opinions of others.

Communication: not pulling any surprises.

Sacrifice: giving your time; understanding that there is no *I* in *TEAM*.

Support: the willingness to provide assistance, when asked; the right to expect assistance, when requested.

Cooperation: showing respect to peers and authority figures; tolerance.

Students must be taught that both musical and non-musical things are equally important for success...they are two sides of the same coin.

B. Music Fundamentals

This component encompasses the development of fundamental aural, dexterous, and interpretive skills/concepts. The primary objective is the progressive development of "common ground" fundamentals, or elements applicable to the performance of most types of music. For organizational and instructional clarity, this component can be divided into *areas of concentration:*

75

- Instrument/Voice Care *(preventive maintenance)*

- Tone Production *(making every note beautiful)*

- Reading Skills *(reading notes and rhythms as proficiently as you read letters and words)*
  - Notation/Theory
  - Key awareness
  - Immediate recognition & accurate response to notes/pitches
  - Immediate recognition & accurate response to rhythms
  - Technical proficiency

- Articulation/Diction *(clarity of text/style)*

- Internal Pulse *(feeling the pulse, not thinking the pulse)*

- Ear Training *("listening" vs. "hearing")*
  - Unisons/Octaves: blending, tuning, balancing

- Chords: blending, tuning, balancing
  - Interval tuning
■ Expression (making music speak)

Although this is in no way a closed list, progressive development of these areas provides a solid foundation for tackling most music-making projects.

Practical Application

Resist the temptation to begin your rehearsals with a mundane routine of thoughtlessly blazing through long tones, arpeggios, "comfort" scales, etc. Instead, use the warm-up portion of your rehearsals as a workshop for developing key fundamentals. Employ thoughtfully chosen exercises that will compliment and directly benefit current performance literature. Not only is this approach filled with purpose, it allows you to get more accomplished and enables your students to see a direct connection between fundamentals and "real" music-making projects.

Example

Your rehearsal plans for the day center around the preparation of a musical work that is in the key of F major and 3/4 time. The majority of the work is to be performed in a smooth, connected style with much rubato. To accentuate these elements and key fundamentals, begin the rehearsal with the following exercises:

Exercise 1

Long tones in the key of F major.

Focus: Factors that contribute to the production of beautiful tones and non-verbal communication (not the specific exercise itself).

By cueing every pitch (a.k.a. rubato), students will have to keep their eyes on you in order to move together.

Exercise 2

Using the same tones performed in Exercise 1, perform 3 legato quarter per pitch with much rubato.

Focus: Factors that contribute to the production of beautiful tones and non-verbal communication (not the specific exercise itself).

Exercise 3

Scales/Arpeggios—at least one of which is in the key of F major.

Focus: Accurate pitches, articulation/diction, and pre-cision (not the specific exercise itself).

Emphasize clarity of style through contrast; when ascending, perform in a smooth, connected style; when descending, per-form in a light, separated style.

Exercise 4

Sight-read new material that is all or partially in the key of F major and in 3/4 time. This could be from a method book, a sight-reading book, or a collection of etudes.

Focus: Reading skills and internal pulse.

Exercise 5

Perform a chorale in the key of F major.

Focus: Ear Training and expression.
This also can be used to emphasize rubato.

 Variations of this example are endless. With just a little thought and planning, the warm-up portion of each rehearsal can easily become a window of meaningful developmental opportunities.

C. Meaningful Application

Musicianship can be applied to a variety of worthwhile music making projects, including performing, composing, arranging, and improvising. In the world of school music ensembles, learning to interpret and perform musical works is obviously a student's primary type of music making. As directors of these ensembles, it is our responsibility to make this process as meaningful (substantial, significant, constructive) as possible. Each music-making project should advance musicianship as well as heighten the realization that music can be an exceptional and lifelong source of personal enjoyment, growth, and discovery.

This brings up an important point. Meaningful music-making experiences do not result from haphazardly selecting two or three tunes, spending weeks and weeks drilling notes and rhythms, cutting parts to cover up a few intonation nightmares, preaching about performing with dynamics, and then BAM!, putting on a concert. In contrast, the total experience of learning to interpret and perform musical works becomes uniquely meaningful by offering students a continuous cycle of music-making experiences that are focused on *quality, diversity,* and *equilibrium.*

Quality: Artistic performance of great musical literature

❒ Artistic Performance

To achieve a genuinely artistic performance, musical works must not only be performed well, but they must also be performed in accordance with the standards and traditions of the musical domain of which they are a part.[35] This requires "performing with understanding,"[36] or exploration beyond the notes and rhythms into the many dimensions, or layers, of musical information that a particular work may embrace.

79

❒ The Quest for the Best

The importance of selecting musical works that reflect and represent the best thinking of a particular musical genre is no secret. Great literature holds great potential for teaching and learning all dimensions of musicianship. Simply put, the music that you present to your students is the sun, the moon, and the stars of the program. Accordingly, the music selection process deserves much thought and attention. Under no circumstances should music be chosen in "the heat of the moment." The important first step to take in making wise musical decisions is taking time to ask questions such as the following:

Does the composition give each performer a sense of individual importance in contributing to the whole?

Are there new skills/concepts that can be introduced in the piece?

Are there previously learned skills/concepts that can be reinforced in the piece?

Does the music favor the ensemble's instrumentation?

Is the music conceived along horizontal lines, rather than always vertical?

Are individual parts and lines transparent? Will the music attract interest on the first hearing?

Does the music have anything to say? Is it worth being said?

80

Choosing music is the single most important thing a [music] director can do....The music we choose today can affect students forever.

-Frederick Fennell-

The most important key to the success of any performing ensemble lies in the quality of its repertoire.

-Donald Hunsberger-

Diversity: Performing/studying music that is representative of varied musical styles.

Music is a universal language that has evolved over centuries, and there are many musical horizons to encounter. By studying a diverse musical palette, you are:

- Helping students to develop a more concise perspective of music's evolution and place throughout the world.

- Increasing the likelihood that students will discover a style or type of music that "speaks their language." A single, unique work could be the spark that ignites a close and lasting relationship with music that might otherwise never have been discovered.

- Bringing the performer in direct contact with thoughts, ideas, and expressions of emotion from a completely different generation of people.

- Engaging students in true multi-cultural experiences.

81

- Offering students opportunities to develop different types of performance skills.

Practical Application

Expose your students to an abundance of literature. *There is significant value in even modest exposure to great works of music, and every composition that you present to your students does not have to be performed outside of the rehearsal.* Steady musical growth, as well as sustained interest for music making, requires far more than just a couple of "concert or contest" tunes. When constructing a musical course of study, consider including the following:

❐ Study Works
Study works are compositions of the utmost quality that are used for in-depth study and preparation. These

selections should be the centerpieces of the curriculum and must be chosen with great care and thought. Study works are typically the compositions performed at contests and festivals.

❏ Performance Works
Performance works are well-crafted pieces used for public performances. These selections are artistically prepared, but because of time constraints, will not be explored to the extent of study works.

❏ Exposure Works

Exposure works are compositions that are chosen to give students, at the very least, the opportunity to read some of the many great musical works that are available for all stages of development. These works are selected for classroom performance only.

 Since a primary value of music is enjoyment, it only makes sense that the process of acquiring musicianship should be enjoyable as well. Including music that represents the culture in which your students are a part can be a highly effective tool for making this happen. It is only natural for students to enjoy performing music that is reflective of their time and place in this world. Most students already have the know-how to derive meaning from many of the musical dimensions present in con-temporary music. The growth and enjoyment achieved through the performance/study of this music can then be used as a step-ping stone into other musical practices.

By incorporating a variety of *performance media* into your program, the task of exposing students to diverse musical styles becomes much easier. This also provides additional avenues for the exploration of forms of musicing other than performing (i.e. composing, arranging, improvising, and conducting).

❒ Concert Ensembles
Concert ensembles are the "heart" of all great programs, and they provide an exceptional setting for musical teaching and learning. Make use of the vast amount of quality repertoire available for truly meaningful music-making experiences.

❒ Jazz Ensembles
The jazz idiom offers many opportunities for rich music-making projects. One of the most important opportunities that it provides is improvisation. Improvisation is music-making in its purest form and should not be avoided. Students are generally much more receptive to this when it is introduced at an early age.

❒ Chamber Ensembles
Performing in a small ensemble is a tremendous means for students to engage in rewarding music making. Because everyone has an independent part and every part is equally important to the overall performance, small ensembles are excellent vehicles for getting students excited about performing, inspiring them to practice, helping them to acquire a genuine love for music, and motivating them in general. Furthermore, good ensemble playing develops essential qualities such as cooperation, teamwork, and tolerance.[37]

❒ Pep Ensembles
The opportunity to perform at school and community

events is an opportunity for meaningful application. For example, sporting events provide a prime setting for up-beat, contemporary music that students and audiences generally enjoy. There are usually large numbers of spectators, and students are seen and heard by several factions of people. This in itself is meaningful to most students. They are performing music representative of the time and place in which they live, for a purpose, and to an audience. If the music is being performed well, and it was a balanced challenge to begin with, students are also demonstrating their increased musicianship. The whole of the experience, as much as one may hate it, is constructive. The key is balance. When pep ensembles are just one part of a diverse performing schedule (one piece of the performance puzzle), there is justifiable merit in their existence.

 Performing well at school and community events (e.g. parades, basketball games, town fairs, faculty meetings) promotes school spirit and models high achievement. These are two key bargaining chips for continued and/or improved funding and support.

❐ Marching Band
Although it is often at the center of controversy, the performance medium known as marching band can be a highly effective means of providing students with significant musical challenges. Musicianship develops best in authentic, action-based teaching/learning situations, and with thoughtful planning, the marching band can be transformed into a vehicle for authentic induction into many different musical practices. The legends, lore, costumes, performance traditions, purposes, occasions and settings of various musical

practices can all be brought to life, or simulated, through the marching band idiom. Unfortunately, the marching band is seldom used for this purpose. Stumbling through a parade or field show playing the latest pop hit, or whatever was on sale last weekend at the music store, is not the idea. Another issue is obviously resources (i.e. funds, staff, time, facilities). Elaborate productions require a substantial commitment from all parties concerned, but when the resources are available, this medium can provide students with compelling music-making challenges and meaningful educational experiences.

85

 At the end of each month, ask yourself, "What did my students learn?" If the answer is something like, "How to perform most of the notes and rhythms in two contest tunes," then it's time to ask yourself another question: "Why do I do what I do?"

Equilibrium: Matching music and musician.

In *Music Matters,* David J. Elliot presents a "praxial" philosophy of music and music education. This philosophy proposes that in addition to the many purposes for which music is made (dancing, worshiping, celebrating, marching, mourning, socializing, teaching, and learning), there are also the underlying central values that music making provides as a human pursuit. Elliot explains that several interdependent tendencies of human consciousness help to clarify the interests that human beings take in making and listening to music:

First, it seems characteristic of human beings that we deploy our powers of consciousness not merely to survive but to understand. As Aristotle said, we "desire to know." Humans seek to understand who they are and what they are capable of doing. We have an innate propensity to bring order to consciousness and to gain self-knowledge.

Second, we tend to enjoy pursuits that extend our capacities. Humans enjoy (and seek further enjoyment in) pursuits that they find absorbing, demanding, and self-fulfilling. We are motivated to understand more. We relish pursuits that challenge our abilities and fully engage our powers of consciousness. It is characteristic of human beings that we do things for the sake of the self-growth that arises from investing our powers of consciousness in the actions of a challenging pursuit.[38]

In this view, the *actions* of music making and music-listening are inherently valuable as a unique and major source of self-growth, self-knowledge (or constructive knowledge), and enjoyment (or "flow"). Furthermore, experiencing these values also contributes to the ongoing development of self-esteem and happiness.[39]

The key here is that a challenge is what sets self-growth and enjoyment in motion. As Elliot explains, there is considerable agreement among cognitive scientists that the prerequisite for self-growth and optimal experience is a match, or at least a balance, between something a person conceives or regards as a challenge and the know-how that person brings to the challenging situation.

Any form of intentional activity (including musicing) to which there is a corresponding form of know-how provides the basis for ordering consciousness and experiencing enjoyment. Enjoyment is not something that just happens; enjoyment is something that people make happen as a result of their efforts to meet the demands of something that they themselves deem a challenge. [40]

Thus, the values of self-growth, self-knowledge, enjoyment, and self-esteem arise when a person's level of musicianship matches a given musical challenge (i.e. musical works to interpret, perform, improvise, compose, arrange, or conduct). Tackling and solving appropriately matched musical challenges advances musicianship and brings students into contact with the "internal goods" of music making. [41]

When a person's level of musicianship matches a given musical challenge, his or her powers of consciousness are completely engaged. Consciousness and action merge to take us up into the actions of musicing. Music making done well (according to artistic obligations of a musical practice) engages the whole self. Music making is valuable and significant in itself because it propels the self to higher levels of complexity. As a student's level of musicianship progresses in complexity to meet the demands of increasingly

intricate works, all aspects of consciousness are likewise propelled upward. [42]

The message is clear. The repertoire that we present to
our students must be well within their musical reach;
it must be matched in terms of musical and technical
demands to their present level of musical "know-how."
As Robert C. Rowlins puts it, "The vast majority of
musical assignments that students encounter must
lie within, but at the verge of, their capabilities. [43]
H. Robert Reynolds (University of Michigan) agrees:

88

> Our job as music educators includes
> helping [performers] to achieve more
> technical ability, but it certainly
> does not stop there. We teach technique
> to serve the music, so we can engage
> the students in heightened and deeper
> musical experiences. In my estimation,
> this goal is best achieved when the
> music is not too difficult. [44]

This proposition makes perfect sense. In fact,
engaging students in an appropriate succession of
learning materials is basic to success in many disci-
plines. For example, when my sons were learning to
read, their first books were very short and simple. They
started with *Brown Bear, Brown Bear,* and with each
new book, took on bigger words, longer text and
eventually made the transition to "chapter" books.
After conquering one level, they were eager to move
on to the next, having readily experienced success.
They could simply sit down and read, perhaps asking
for help with a word or two, and grasp the meaning of

the story. If throughout this process they had encountered too many books that were over their heads,
frustration would have set in. Likewise, if they had
encountered too many books that were overly simplistic,
boredom would have set in. In either case, their interest
and ability in reading would not be close to what it
is today.

The same principle applies to music education.
Music-making experiences become much more meaningful and productive when there is an appropriate
match between the musician and the musical challenge.
A continuous cycle of solving (artistically performing)
appropriately-balanced musical works propels musicianship forward, prepares the learner for increasingly
complex musical challenges, and brings forth the many
enriching virtues that music-making has to share.

To put it another way, the values of music-making
arise by performing well (meeting all of the technical
and musical demands inherent in a given musical
work). In order for this to occur, the musical work must
be within the students' musical and technical reach.
When a piece is too difficult—unattainable within a
reasonable amount of practice time—frustration will
result. When a piece is too easy, boredom will result. In
either case, musicianship will not be significantly
advanced, if at all, and the experience as a whole will
not bring the performers into contact with the "internal
goods" of music-making.

Practical Application
❏ The 80/20 Principle

Invest wisely in your students' musical growth by

offering a diverse musical portfolio that is essentially 80% readily attainable and 20% appropriately challenging. This proposition has a three-way translation, which is best explained in context:

> Out of ten pieces of music, for example, eight should be readily attainable in terms of difficulty and demand for the vast majority of students in the ensemble. The other two pieces should offer a reasonable musical stretch (e.g. expanded range, technical demands, key signatures, rhythm patterns, meters, forms), and should fall under the 80/20 principle as well: 80% of the students in the ensemble should be able to readily execute 80% of the musical and technical demands.

90

By choosing works that students can readily perform—music within their musical reach and in line with the 80/20 principle—there won't be the need to spend large amounts of rehearsal time pounding notes and rhythms. This alone has several important advantages:

- You have time to expand your instructional dimensions. You can teach your students how to *perform with understanding,* which in turn contributes to the development of "comprehensive musicianship." (See also *Performing With Understanding,* page 100)

- You have more time to perform more music (See also *Diversity,* page 80).

- You don't have to stop as much. You can teach broader concepts that encompass larger sections of the piece. Naturally, this cuts down on discipline issues because students are engaged in music-making for longer periods of time.

The values of music making arise in the actions of interpreting and performing musical works (real live music-making), not in the actions of rehearsing, or preparing to perform (start . . . stop . . . sit a while).

❏ Be patient

If a grade III piece is required for a particular contest, and your students are realistically at a grade I, then the task is obviously to bring the group to the point where grade III music can be artistically performed. To accomplish this, fight the urge to pass out a grade III piece and drill it to death. Regardless of how great a piece of music may be, if you run it into the ground, students will quickly lose interest. Instead, begin with "Brown Bear, Brown Bear" and slowly introduce works at level I+, II, and II+. Before you know it, your students will be ready and eager for level III. If time won't allow this, maybe you should reconsider the value of taking your students to that particular event. Perhaps taking them to a different contest, one in which they can perform music at their actual level, is a more edu-cationally-sound alternative.

91

 This alternative should only be a temporary solution. There is definite merit in achieving the levels set forth by your state association or other organizations such as MENC. These levels were not randomly established; they reflect performance levels that students of certain stages should be at from extensive research and experience.

❏ Students should be grouped by ability, not grade.

This is important because no two students progress at

the same rate. After the first year, or even the first semester, students matched by grade will also more than likely be mismatched in ability. In turn, the musical projects will automatically be too simple or too hard, resulting in boredom and/or frustration. Thus, whenever possible, students should be grouped by their degree of musicianship, not their ages.

In conclusion, musicianship does not develop by happenstance! Comprehensive musical training requires:

92

A. An environment conducive to teaching and learning.

B. Thorough grounding in key music fundamentals.

C. A carefully-balanced, hands-on tour of meaningful music-making projects: *the artistic performance of an abundant palette of quality literature that is varied in style and within the students' musical reach.*

Part II: Independent Study

Independent study is important because music is so vast...there is so much to learn, explore, and discover. The goal here is to give students the opportunity to pursue specific aspects of music that are especially interesting or helpful to them. This is also known as "enrichment."

Practical Application

❏ The Nine Weeks Project

This is a long-term, music-related activity that is

selected by the student and should be completed over each nine-week grading period. If there are huge numbers of students involved, this could easily be converted into a "Semester Project." Nevertheless, the possibilities are endless:

- Solos (to be performed at a festival/contest/concert).

 Allow students to select their own solo music. This gives them an opportunity to make musical decisions on their own, as well as to learn to make judgments on the quality of the music they have selected. Was it worth the effort or not?

93

- Participate in a duet, trio, or other small ensemble (to be performed at a festival/contest/concert).
- Audition for an honor's group.
- An extended-practice assignment targeted at developing specific fundamentals, such as improving sight-reading skills, building technique, or expanding range (i.e. learning all of the major or minor scales, practicing a series of sight-reading exercises followed by a sight-reading test).
- Study with a jazz musician to learn or refine improvisation skills.
- Give private lessons to younger students in the program.
- Learn to sing a piece written in a different language (i.e. Italian, German).
- Write, arrange, or rearrange a piece of music for a specific instrument/voice.
- Compose, arrange, or rearrange a piece of music for a small ensemble.
- Compose, arrange, or rearrange a piece of music for full band/orchestra/choir.
- Conduct/rehearse a small ensemble (including a performance).

- Conduct/rehearse the band/orchestra/choir (including a performance).
- Complete a music-theory workbook or software course.
- Prepare a report about a specific time, place, or person in music history that is connected to a work being studied.
- Prepare a report on a composer who is connected to a work being studied.
- Learn how to play a new instrument (e.g. violin to viola, baritone to tuba).
- Learn how to make and adjust reeds.

94

Use this list as a springboard for creating your own list of **assignments and projects that encourage the kind of learning that you want students to achieve.**

Independent study projects can also be effective vehicles for implementing remedial work. If a student is seriously behind in his/her musical development, you can assign specific exercises that target the student's most pressing needs as part (or even all) of his/her nine-week project.

Part III: The Mastery Learning Model

Insanity is doing the same thing year after year and expecting different results.

In a perfect world, all of our students would be taking private lessons, and the median level of musicianship within each section would be similar to and at the upper end of proficiency. Unfortunately, we all know this is not the case. A close examination into the levels of musicianship present in most groups would reveal wide variance. Furthermore, the majority of students would not be in the upper percentile. There are several possible reasons for this:

- Music directors often have large numbers of students to teach and very little time, proportionately, to do it. This makes it difficult to give students the attention they deserve.
- Performance demands are often extreme. This puts students and directors constantly "under the gun," which makes the process more survival-oriented than achievement-oriented.
- Expectations and standards are low. Students are not motivated to practice on their own.
- In larger districts, there is often a lack of consistency from school to school and/or from director to director.
- In smaller districts, the entire program is often run by a single director, and finding time to keep up with everything (including tutoring students who need extra help) is an overwhelming task.

95

Fortunately, there is a solution to this problem. It's called *Mastery Learning,* and it can do great things for any music program.

The Mastery Learning Model was introduced by Dr. Benjamin S. Bloom (University of Chicago) in his article "Learning for Mastery." According to Bloom, "...the basic underlying ideas [of Mastery Learning] have been known for over 2000 years by leading educators from the time of Plato and Socrates to that of Morrison and Washburne in the early years of the twentieth century."[45] Mastery Learning is basically a *group-based* and teacher-paced instructional process that creates a manageable, effective, instructional framework. As Thomas R. Guskey explains, "it involves organizing instruction, providing students with regular feedback on their learning progress, giving guidance and direction to help students correct their individual learning difficulties, and providing extra challenges for students who have mastered the material."[46]

Why should the Mastery Learning process be used in music programs?

- Mastery Learning is a proven means of achieving results close to that of one-on-one tutoring or private lessons with a large group of students. According to Bloom, "the general finding is that the average student under mastery learning exceeds the level of learning of about 85 percent of the students learning the same subject under conventional instructional conditions—*even with the same teacher.*"[47]

- "In essence, Mastery Learning provides teachers with a way to better *individualize* teaching and learning within a group-based classroom."[48]

- Mastery Learning involves organizing instruction into learning units. A unit is a specific group of objectives with corresponding activities and strategies to achieve them. This process of organization helps to clarify specific learning goals for students, which increases student achievement. Think of a series of units as a pathway to summative learning goals and outcomes.

- Mastery Learning is a means of providing all students with appropriate instruction. It's no secret that different students learn in different ways. In the mastery-learning process, students are given correctives that are tailored to their dominant style of learning.

- The Mastery Learning Model allows the music director to concentrate on all students, not just the top or bottom of each section.

- Mastery Learning is a teaching/learning process that is sensitive to large groups and limited instructional time.

- Mastery Learning allows teachers to help nearly all of their students become much more successful in learning. When students are successful in learning, the doors to self-confidence and self-esteem open wide and suddenly school isn't such a bad place to be after all.

The following are brief discussions and practical applications of the major components involved in mastery learning:

1) Instructional Units and Objectives
2) Instructional Input
3) Formative Tests
4) Correctives & Enrichment
5) Summative Exams

Mastery Learning Component 1: Instructional Units and Objectives

In the Mastery Learning Model, the material that is to be learned over the course of a semester or year is divided into smaller learning units, which contain *specific learning objectives.* In the context of school music ensembles, the time between each performance creates a natural learning unit, or performance unit. The exact length of each unit can be adjusted to accommodate your specific needs and circumstances. However, research has proven that the shorter the task, the greater the rate of success; the longer the task, the greater the rate of failure.[49]

*This point further validates the importance of **not** spending week after week drilling the same two compositions.*

Practical Application
- -
Establish the primary objectives, or learning goals, for each performance unit. Students must know precisely what they are expected to learn.

Examples
- Fulfillment of specific personal responsibilities and rehearsal procedures.
- Development of specific fundamental skills/concepts.
- In-depth exploration and preparation of specific *study works.*
- Preparation of specific *performance works.*
- Reading specific *exposure works.*

Daily rehearsal plans can be created and revised throughout the course of each performance unit. Specific learning needs and teaching plans arise in the actions of teaching, not weeks ahead of time.

Establish **weekly practice units** that consist of specific materials for individual practice. These could include just about anything; however, *home-practice assignments should be directly related to the materials being worked on in class.* Congruence among instructional components is essential for mastery learning. It is also helpful for practice units to run from Monday to Monday. This gives students a weekend of practice time after a week of guided practice.

Example
- Page 17 in the method book (dotted-eighth note study)
- Measures 1-48 in *Prelude and Dance*
- Measures 36-72 in *1st Suite*

99

Mastery Learning Component 2: Instructional Input

This is where instructional strategies are applied towards the accomplishment of specific learning objectives. In other words, this is the part where you actually teach. Although this book is not aimed at specific instructional strategies, the following five principles deserve mention because they are universal and applicable to virtually all musical teaching/learning situations.

 The terms "conductor" and "music educator" are synonymous. You can't be one without being the other.

1) *Great conductors are musical mirrors.* Their musical wishes are reflected in their actions. They do not just conduct beats, they conduct music. Their gestures and body language emphasize "how" the music should be performed, not just "when" the music should be performed.[50]

2) *Great conductors are master storytellers.* They awaken the mind by connecting musical thoughts and ideas to things in everyday life; they paint vivid, imaginative, mental images that students can immediately relate to. Why? To capture the performer's attention and help him or her become more absorbed in listening and reacting to others. Great conductors know that "minds in concert," or performing together by thinking together, is a fundamental, irreducible constituent of truly superior performances.

100

3) *Great conductors help students to "perform with understanding."* They offer insight into relative, interesting facts and concepts that surround the work being studied. They not only teach "how," they teach "why" and "about." They provide connections between the music and the people, places, things, beliefs, ideas, values, legends, lore, customs, and traditions that surround the work; they provide answers to these types of questions:

- *Who wrote the piece? When? Where? Why?*
- *Does the work tell a story? What is it?*
- *What was going on in the world when the piece was written?*
- *What style/type/form of music is the work representative of?*
- *What are the unique musical characteristics of the piece?*
- *What images or emotions does the work invoke?*
- *What is the purpose of studying the piece?*

4) *Great conductors are more musically inclined than mechanically inclined.* They teach mechanical elements only to serve the music and to empower

performers to express the music to its fullest potential. They are primarily concerned with "making the
music speak," and the vast majority of their energy is
devoted to issues such as the shape of musical lines,
blending of colors, phrasing, and nuance. Theirs is a
process of creation, not mindless repetition, and
"reading the story" is of much greater importance
than "correcting the grammar."[51] To put it another
way, great conductors are not merely fixers, they
are builders. Although the "fix it" approach
*(rehearse until something goes wrong . . . stop . . .
fix it)* is very common, it is considerably lacking in
purpose. As Richard Floyd explains, "One must
never regard notes, rhythms, and other technical
aspects as ends in themselves. These components
are only the necessities that enable one to make
music."[52] H. Robert Reynolds supports this view with
a unique analogy: "Too many teachers are teaching
young students to follow the marks...Following the
marks is like painting by the numbers, and one is
not having any artistic experience through that kind
of 'painting.' It is better to have an image of a bird
in your head and paint that than it is to paint the
bird by the numbers, even if one alters the shades
of the colors."[53] It all comes down to a choice. You
can teach students to perform for today, or you
can engineer rehearsals to illuminate the creative
and expressive aspects of music that will enrich
their tomorrows.

101

5) *Great conductors utilize natural forces to help
    performers reach their full potential.* Musicianship
    is essentially a matter of procedural knowledge—
    knowing *how,* not knowing *that*—and *The Natural*

Learning Process (a title coined by W. Timothy Gallwey) is a highly-effective method of learning how to do something that all of us, including our students, have been perfecting since birth. This innate capacity is how we all learned to walk and talk, and involves mental imagery, imitation, repetition via trial-and-error practice, and internal/external feedback. In *Musical Performance,* Daniel L. Kohut defines these elements as follows: [54]

102

> **Mental Imagery** = *the imaginary pictures we create in our minds of tasks or goals.*
>
> **Imitation** = *our attempt to duplicate mental images.*
>
> **Repetition via trial-and-error practice** = *the process we use to target and solve problems.*
>
> **Internal Feedback** = *kinesthetic (physical sensations) and vestibular (body balance) information.*
>
> **External Feedback** = *information obtained from our senses and input from others.*

In the Natural Learning Process, all that is required to learn is a good model to imitate and repetition that is fueled by desire. In fact, the very essence of this type of learning is focusing on the goal, not the process. [55] When using the Natural Learning Process in the context of teaching and learning music, our primary task as teachers is to flood our students' minds with superior musical images for them to duplicate. As Arnold Jacobs explains, "The focus of our teaching should be on training the performer's brain. We can't really train the muscles; we train the brain, which controls the muscles." [56]

Once a clear mental picture of the performance goal is obtained, the next step is to simply allow the body's neuromuscular functions to take over and achieve it. The details of the process are left up the the body, and as Kohut points out, we are all more than capable of handling this:

> ...everyone who inhabits a human body possesses an absolutely marvelous piece of mechanical, chemical, and electrical equipment. Contrary to what most people seem to believe, it is quite capable of executing many complex functions on its own without any conscious direction from us. It was designed to operate this way. When we give it too many instructions, we only interfere with its superior capability and confuse, confound, and jam up its intricate mechanisms; thus causing it to perform poorly. The fewer the instructions we give it, the better. The primary instruction our body needs [on a conscious level] is specification of the general musical goal, not a detailed set of instructions on how to achieve that goal.[57]

103

Unfortunately, as simple and effective as this process is, a slight problem exists. As teachers, we often load our students down with so much irrelevant information that this natural process is completely obliterated by unnatural forces.

> ...the main problem with imitative teaching today is that too few teachers actually teach this way. Music teachers, for example, rely mainly on verbal description and physiological analysis as the primary means toward teaching musical performance skills as well as musical expression. If repeated verbal description and analysis fail to achieve results, one is then likely to see the teacher

exasperatingly either sing or play the passage, as if singing or playing it for the student were the last resort! But since music is a nonverbal form of artistic expression, trying to teach it primarily through verbal description and analysis goes against all sense of reasonable logic. We should be doing just the opposite — teaching nonverbal concepts through nonverbal means. To reinforce this idea, a quote from Gallwey seems appropriate here: "Images are better than words, showing better than telling, too much instruction worse than none, and conscious trying often produces negative results." [58]

104

The message here is that students do not need long-winded verbal explanations to learn how to make music. What they do need is superior *musical models* to imitate (through live demonstrations and exemplary recordings), help with focusing on the musical goal (not the process), and opportunities to target and solve performance problems using their own sensory feedback (repetition).

`An aural picture is worth a thousand words.`

`Einstein...was asked if example is the best way to teach; he answered, "No, it's the only way to teach."` [59]

Intimately related to The Natural Learning Process are the *Inner Game* techniques proposed by W. Timothy Gallwey. The NLP and the Inner Game are essentially two sides of the same coin. Both are aimed at learning from our own experience.

In *The Inner Game of Music* by Barry Green (with W. Timothy Gallwey), Green explains the following "Inner Game Basics" and how they can be used to improve the process of teaching and learning music:

The Performance Equation:
(P)Performance = (p)Potential – (i)Interference.

By reducing Interference **(i),** our Performance **(P)** comes closer to our true Potential **(p).**

Self 1 and Self 2. The little voice inside our heads suggests that there's a talker and there's a listener. Gallwey refers to the voice doing the talking as Self 1, and the person spoken to as Self 2. Self 1 is our interference and functions to give commands (specify performance goals) to Self 2.[60] The function of Self 2 is to execute commands given by Self 1. "Self 2 is the vast reservoir of potential within each of us. It contains our natural talents and abilities, and is a virtually unlimited resource that we can tap and develop. Left to its own devices, it performs with gracefulness and ease."[61] Gallwey sums up the importance of identifying Self 1 and Self 2 as follows: If it interferes with your potential, it's Self 1. If it expresses your potential, it's Self 2.[62]

The ultimate challenge of the Inner Game is to eliminate the critical interference of Self 1 and unleash the natural power and boundless potential of Self 2.[63] As teachers, one of the greatest gifts we can give our students is help in meeting this challenge, and a great place to begin is with the Inner Game skill of *awareness.* As Green explains, awareness is an "antidote to trying," which often fails. It is a simple and extremely powerful way to direct our concentration, cope with mental and other distractions, and bring us closer to realizing our full potential. By focusing our attention on one element of the present moment, we relax out of our "trying" mode and allow our conscious mind to listen to what's really happening. This increases the amount of feedback we receive and permits the body to implement positive changes almost effortlessly.[64]

106 In short, awareness helps us keep our focus on the desired musical goal, not the process.

The key to helping students increase their awareness is to avoid "do this, do that" instructions and compliment repetition (trial-and-error practice), with *"awareness instructions."*

> *Awareness instructions put students into an entirely different frame of mind [than "do this, do that" instructions]. They are based on the students' own experience—their ability to learn by noticing what's happening. They don't involve "right" or "wrong" ways to go about things. They don't involve a complex series of steps that are easily confused or forgotten. They never demand more of the body than it is capable of handling. They don't invoke doubt. And as a result, they free students from doubt, confusion, frustration, and discouragement.[65]*

Changing a "do this, do that" instruction into an awareness instruction requires rephrasing it so that the focus of attention is on the student's experience.[66] Here are some examples offered by Green that can help you better understand and explore this approach.

- Instead of "Draw the bow perpendicular to the bow string," (which can invoke the thought of "I'll try hard to keep it straight") use *"Notice the angle of the bow when the resistance is steady."*

- Instead of "Don't clip your consonants at the ends of phrases," (which can invoke thoughts of "Which phrases?" "How should I pronounce them?" "Why?") use *"Listen to the sound of the consonants at the ends of phrases. See if you can clearly hear the words."*

- Instead of "Play louder as you go to the higher notes," (which invokes the thoughts of "How much louder?" "Which notes are wrong?" "Am I loud enough now?") use *"Pay attention to the degree of increase in volume as you play higher notes."* [67]

107

A key premise of education in general is that no two students learn in exactly the same ways. The Natural Learning Process is a very personal mode of learning. Through focused imitation, repetition, and trial and error practice, students can target and solve performance problems using their own sensory feedback. When combined with a teacher who provides superior mental images and helps them to fulfill their potential by eliminating interference (such as developing the Inner Game skill of awareness), the complete package is almost flawless...*a harmonious synchronization of student, teacher, and Nature.*

Practical Application

■ Program your students' brains with superior musical images.

■ Allow students to re-create, or imitate, the musical images you have given them via trial-and-error practice.

■ Give students time to target and solve performance problems on their own using internal and external feedback.

■ Compliment repetition with *awareness instructions.* Avoid "do this, do that" statements. Focus student awareness on something in the *present moment* that will help them to pay attention to their own experience and the desired musical goal, not the process.

108

- *"Let's see if you can pinpoint exactly where the music is slowing down (or speeding up)."*
- *"Be aware of your air stream. Does it feel free and flowing, or tight and restricted?"*
- *"Notice if this passage sounds like only one instrument is playing."*
- *"Notice if your notes are longer or shorter than those around you."*
- *"Can you feel the music pulling you towards measure nine?"*
- *"See if you're still playing when there's a rest in the music."*
- *"Notice if you're holding each note for the correct number of pulses (subdivisions)."*
- *"Can you tell which note in this phrase is not being held long enough?"*
- *"As you sing the phrase, notice if you feel as if you are being lifted up and then lowered back down."*

Mastery Learning Component 3: Formative Tests

After the material of an instructional unit is presented, periodic formative tests are given to check on learning progress. The purpose of a formative test is to provide precise feedback to both the teacher and student about what has been learned well, or mastered, and what has not. Formative tests also provide the teacher with opportunities to offer the student specific suggestions for correcting any learning difficulties. In other words, "formative tests are both diagnostic and prescriptive. They help students identify their specific learning difficulties and provide individualized prescriptions for reaching mastery of the material in the unit." [68]

Practical Application

An effective means of formative testing within a performance group setting is the *"mini-performance quiz."* This is a brief performance demonstration over a short segment of music. "Mini-quizzes" should be given as often as practical, with the evaluation material taken directly from the current weekly practice unit. The term "mini-quiz" is used as an alternative to "test" due to the negative connotations that this word often brings.

109

There are several ways of implementing these "live" performance assessments within the rehearsal setting:

Option A: Listen to each individual perform the material in a sequential rotation. Simply select who will start, and tell the rest of the students that their turn begins as soon as the person next to them finishes.

This procedure is very easily learned. You can listen to approximately eight students per minute perform a 2-3 measure segment at a moderate tempo. If the group is extremely large, you can split this up (i.e. sopranos/altos one day, tenors/basses the next).

Option B: Listen to small groups (i.e. sections, parts) perform the material. If it is evident during this performance that even one person in the group is not prepared, immediately motion for the group to stop and proceed with Option A. Each group should receive the same opportunity to perform the material collectively first.

This option offers the security of performing with others and additional incentive for each individual to be really prepared. No one wants to be the reason each member of the group has to repeat the material.

Option C: Listen to pairs of students perform the material. This approach, as does option B, includes the bonus of requiring proper intonation in addition to notes, rhythms, etc.

110

At first glance, it might appear that this type of assessment is musically unhealthy because it puts students "on the spot." However, in addition to the fact that it is very impractical to give frequent performance quizzes in a private setting, there are significant advantages to this means of evaluation. Consistent use, especially when started during early stages of instruction, makes performing in front of others a normal part of rehearsals, or "what real musicians do...not a once-in-a-while momentous occasion which makes or breaks the student's grade [or confidence]."[69] This mode of assessment also provides increased motivation for serious practice. Not only will students be practicing for results and grades, they will also be practicing to perform well in front of their peers.

With even moderate amounts of planning, it is quite possible to give formative tests to younger (middle school) students almost daily. Although the performance calendar often prohibits this degree of frequency with high school students, there are very few good reasons, if any, for not fitting an occasional performance quiz into your rehearsal plans. Simply post a weekly practice assignment that is connected to your current performance projects and squeeze in a short quiz from time to time. At least once a week is preferable, but even once every other week is better than none at all. With just a little consistency, students quickly realize they will be held accountable for practicing outside of the rehearsal. Not only is this great for individual musical growth, but this strategy also saves time, because rehearsals are so much more productive. In plain terms, "the more frequent th tests, the higher the achievement." [70]

Week 1

Mon	Assign Practice Unit 1
Tue	
Wed	Mini-quiz over 2-3 most rhythmically-complex measures in Practice Unit 1
Thu	
Fri	Mini-quiz over 2-3 most technically-complex measures in Practice Unit 1

Week 2

Mon	Mini-quiz over complete phrase in unit 1; Assign Practice Unit 2

A practical alternative to "live" testing is to have students submit regular recordings of their weekly practice assignments. This also provides recorded proof of accomplishment (or lack of accomplishment). The down side, especially with large groups, is that evaluating such recordings takes considerable time, and it is very easy to fall behind.

A critical element in the mastery learning process is regular, diagnostic, and prescriptive feedback. [71] Consistent use of a *performance assessment tool,* such as the following two examples, can be very helpful in providing students with specific information on what they have learned well and what needs more attention.

Assessment Forms

Name _____ **Date** _____
Selection _____

Posture & Position

0	5	10
Incorrect	*Inconsistent*	*Correct*

Notes, Rhythms, Articulation/Diction

1 2 3 4 5 6 7 8 9 10 11 12 13 14 15 16
17 18 19 20 21 22 23 24 25 26 27 28
29 30 31 32 33 34 35
Performance errors

Tempo

0	5
Inappropriate	*Very Inconsistent*

10	15
Inconsistent	*Appropriate*

Musical Expression
The combination of all musical elements, including markings around the notes, to create expressive phrases.

0	10	15	20
Non-Existent	*Fair*	*Good*	*Excellent*

Tone/Voice Quality

0	10	15	20
Poor	*Fair*	*Good*	*Excellent*

Name _____ **Date** _____
Selection _____

Overall performance is exceptional and worthy of special recognition.
___ You performed all of the notes/rhythms/
    articulations correctly
___ Appropriate choice of tempo(s)
___ You artistically incorporated all of the markings
    around the notes into your performance
___ Your performance was very expressive

[ ]   **95-100**

Overall performance is excellent.
___You performed the vast majority of the notes/
    rhythms/articulations correctly
___Appropriate choice of tempo(s)
___You incorporated most of the markings around
    the notes into your performance
___Your performance was moderately expressive

[ ]   **85-94**

Overall performance is of moderately good quality, but less than excellent.
___You performed most of the notes/rhythms/
    articulations correctly
___Acceptable choice of tempo(s)
___You occasionally attempted to incorporate the
    markings around the notes into your performance
___Your performance was moderately expressive at times,
    but inconsistent

[ ]   **75-84**

Overall performance is fair (with few special qualities).
___You performed several of the notes/rhythms/articulations
incorrectly
___Acceptable choice of tempo(s)
___You incorporated very few of the markings around the
notes into your performance
___Your performance was not very expressive

  65-74

Overall performance is poor.
___You performed most of the notes/rhythms/
articulations incorrectly
___Inappropriate choice of tempo(s)
___You did not incorporate any of the markings
around the notes into your performance
___Your performance was not expressive at all

  0-64

Evaluator's Initials_____

Overall Tone Quality

☐ beautiful, characteristic, resonant
☐ full and characteristic at times, inconsistent
☐ Fuzzy, thin, airy, chocked, unsupported, uncharacteristic

 The total points awarded to each caption can be adjusted to fit your specific needs and circumstances. The important issue is to give students specific feedback about their progress.

Feedback and assessment must *encourage the kind of learning that you want students to achieve.* If tests/quizzes are based on notes and rhythms, students will only focus on notes and rhythms. If your tests/quizzes stress musical expression and incorporate all of the markings around the notes, students will be motivated to take notice of these elements as well when they practice.

> Students must be taught to read "around" the notes. I am often reminded of a horse with blinders when I hear students [perform] with no recognition of dynamic markings, accents, or other elements. Their attention is centered only on the individual tone, ignoring the all-important context within which the note exists. [72]
>
> -Edwin Kruth, Emeritus Professor of Music, San Francisco State University-

115

Mastery Learning Component 4: Correctives & Enrichment

Based on the results of the formative test, students who have not mastered all of the material engage in corrective work for a short period of time. Afterwards, and before moving on to the next unit, these students are given a second formative test that covers the same material as the first, but is tailored to the specific needs of the student (i.e. asking questions in a slightly different manner, using a different format). This test is also a powerful motivational tool because it demonstrates to students that they *can* improve their scores and experience success in learning.

For students who demonstrate mastery of the unit material, special enrichment activities are provided. These activities allow fast learners an opportunity to extend their original learning or to become involved in other learning activities that are stimulating and rewarding.

Practical Application

An obvious concern here is not so much how to provide correctives and enrichment, but rather, when and where. In situations where there are two or more directors, students with consistently low scores on performance quizzes can be given extra help, as well as an opportunity to raise their marks, while those who have demonstrated mastery of the material engage in enrichment activities. When only one director is available, several options are possible:

116

• Have students who are excelling work with those who are not (peer tutoring).

This is a form of cooperative learning.

• Meet with students needing extra help outside of regular class time for one-on-one tutoring or small-group practice sessions. Helping each member of a diverse student body overcome learning obstacles often requires time before and/or after school, which, incidentally, is a leading characteristic of those who genuinely make a difference. Besides, for a professional whose ultimate job is to engineer student success, could there be a better reason for going an extra mile?

• Periodically devote a class period exclusively to providing correctives while the rest of the group does a written assignment, watches a music-related video, etc.

Examples of enrichment activities:

✔ Learn new music that is directly related to the materials covered. For example, if learning the Ab concert scale was an objective, pass out a song or solo in this key that you know your students will enjoy performing.

✔ Practice technical exercises twice as fast.

✔ Give "speed tests" for the opportunity to earn extra credit.

✔ Give computer-assisted lessons.

✔ Have students compose and perform a short piece of music that is related to the materials of the unit.

✔ Play a game based on cumulatively-learned materials (i.e. *Who Wants to be a Millionaire or Wheel of Fortune*). Incorporate both questions and live performance. Students love this!

117

Mastery Learning Component 5: Summative Exams

The final step in the Mastery Learning Model is the summative exam. This type of test is much broader based and wider in scope than formative tests, and is generally administered after several units have been covered. The primary purpose of this exam is to assess the criterion objectives of the course and to assign grades.

Practical Application

Examples of summative exams in the context of performance based music courses include:

✔ Participation and performance in concerts and/or contests.

✔ Performance tests in which the student performs excerpts of material studied throughout the grading period.

✔ Written exams over musical terms, forms, styles, etc., studied throughout the grading period.

✔ Sight-reading tests in which the student reads a piece that is similar in style and content to music studied throughout the grading period.

Assessment does not have to be limited to musical elements. It is also important to assess *non-musical attributes*. Behaviors reflective of high character are not only essential for superior achievement in performance-based music ensembles, they are essential to succeeding in life. Being punctual, trustworthy, and capable of working cooperatively with others, for example, are employability traits that will help them to acquire and sustain a good job. Explain to students that by observing and evaluating these things, you are investing in their future.

Examples

■ **Conduct & Participation:** Include cumulative points earned for daily conduct and participation when calculating final marks for each grading period. To help facilitate this, a rubric similar to the one on page 119 can be used for consistency in evaluation and to provide students with specific feedback about their performance.

■ **Character Education:** Provide specific feedback about character-related attributes. This is another area in which the use of an assessment tool can be very beneficial to both student and teacher. Consider using a document similar to the one found on pgs. 120-122 at the end of each semester.

Rehearsal Behavior Rubric [73]

Level 4: The student's attention never wavers from the rehearsal. The student exhibits exceptional behavior, providing a model for others.
20pts/week (+)

Level 3: The student listens attentively, needs no teacher reminders to refrain from talking or interrupting, and follows all the rules for good rehearsal participation.
15pts/week (√)

Level 2: The student needs occasional teacher reminders to listen attentively and/or to refrain from talking, may get out of his/her seat, or does not follow all the rules of good rehearsal participation.
10pts/week (-)

Level 1: The student needs frequent teacher reminders to sit still, refrain from talking, listen attentively, or actively participate. The student makes it difficult for other students to listen. The teacher may move the student to another seat or remove the student from the rehearsal.
5pts/week (0)

Name_____ **Course**_____
Term: 1 2 3 4 5

Confidence
☐ Refuses to perform independently in
front of others
☐ Hesitant to perform independently in
front of others
☐ Volunteers to perform independently in
front of others

☐ Frequently does not want to participate
☐ Readily performs as part of the group
☐ Always eager to participate

Perseverance
☐ Effort quickly diminishes when success is
not immediate, easily distracted
☐ Occasionally distracted, sticks with most
challenges until they are conquered
☐ Learns from mistakes, always remains focused
until challenges are conquered

Preparation
☐ Rarely has all required materials
☐ Occasionally does not have all required materials
☐ Always has all required materials

☐ Rarely begins preparing for class without prompting
☐ Occasionally needs to be prompted to begin
preparing for class
☐ Consistently ready to begin class on time

Dependability
☐ Unpredictable
☐ Attends most performances
☐ Attends all performances

☐ Often late
☐ Occasionally late
☐ Always on time

Task Completion
☐ Has missing assignments
☐ Turns in most assignments
☐ Turns in all assignments

☐ Never meets deadlines
☐ Occasionally misses deadlines
☐ Always meets deadlines, often completes
tasks early

Independent Progress
☐ (Effort to become a better musician)
☐ Minimal progress
☐ Puts forth best effort most of the time
☐ Always puts forth best effort

☐ Little evidence of home practice
☐ Moderate evidence of home practice
☐ Obvious evidence of home practice

☐ Does not seek help
☐ Occasionally seeks help
☐ Always seeks help when needed

Teamwork/Respect
☐ Frequently inattentive
☐ Occasionally inattentive
☐ Always attentive

☐ Rarely follows classroom procedures
☐ Consistently follows most classroom procedures
☐ Consistently follows all classroom procedures

☐ Causes frequent interruptions
☐ Causes occasional interruptions
☐ Never causes any interruptions, always sets a
great example for others

Recommendations
☐ Keep working to elevate areas that need improvement
☐ Make up missing tests and/or turn in missing assignments
☐ Parent/Teacher conference (please call to schedule this)
☐ Private lessons
☐ Conference with counselor

_____

Parent/Guardian Signature

Director's Initials_____

In conclusion, the Mastery Learning Model is an infrastructure for teaching and learning that helps teachers teach more students more of what they are trying to teach. All students deserve an equal chance to succeed! By teaching for mastery, we can become a positive force for making this happen.

As professionals, we all too often make the assumption that public performance is empirical evidence of our effect as teachers. Little could be farther from the truth. [74]

-James Croft-

123

Visual Summary

The following diagram illustrates the final product: a "master plan" for musical teaching and learning which combines the instructional principles, components, tools, and strategies discussed in this section into a versatile *framework* for comprehensive musical teaching and learning. In other words, a blueprint for organizing, implementing, and assessing a progressive series of musical learning experiences within the boundaries, time limitations, and hectic pace of performance-based school music programs.

It is also helpful to consider this instructional framework like a puzzle, with each component representing an individual piece. When combined, the pieces form an enlightening "Musicianship Advancement Plan", or "MAP," which reveals multiple interlocking pathways for enabling all students to achieve and succeed. As with all puzzles, the picture is not complete without each individual piece being in place.

Musicianship Advancement Plan

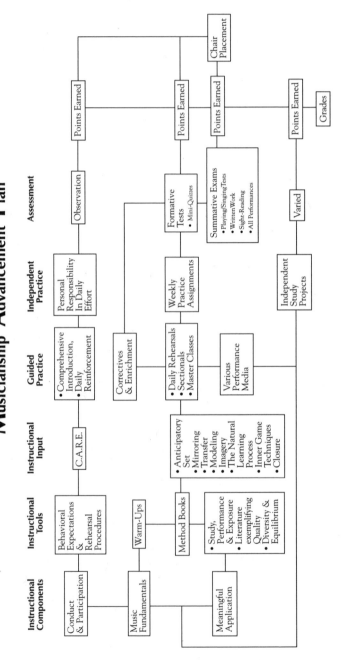

Instructional Components	Instructional Tools	Instructional Input	Guided Practice	Independent Practice	Assessment
Conduct & Participation	Behavioral Expectations & Rehearsal Procedures	C.A.R.E.	• Comprehensive Introduction, • Daily Reinforcement	Personal Responsibility In Daily Effort	Observation → Points Earned → Chair Placement
Music Fundamentals	Warm-Ups		Correctives & Enrichment		
	Method Books	• Anticipatory Set • Mirroring • Transfer • Modeling • Imagery • The Natural Learning Process • Inner Game Techniques • Closure	• Daily Rehearsals • Sectionals • Master Classes	Weekly Practice Assignments	Formative Tests • Mini-Quizzes → Points Earned
Meaningful Application	• Study, Performance & Exposure • Literature exemplifying Quality • Diversity & Equilibrium		Various Performance Media		Summative Exams • Playing/Singing Tests • Written Work • Sight-Reading • All Performances → Points Earned
				Independent Study Projects	Varied → Points Earned → Grades

Additional Benefits of the Musicianship Advancement Plan

Accountable Records

By awarding points and keeping accurate records for daily conduct and participation, formative performance quizzes, summative exams, written work, independent study projects, and participation in required perform- ances (i.e. concerts, festivals, contests), the entire grading process becomes a justifiable reflection of accomplishment and on-going musical growth.

Chair Placement

By keeping a running total of each student's earned **125** points, chair placement can be determined in a completely fair and impartial manner. This strategy awards *total accomplishment* and provides tremen- dous motivation for students to continually strive for excellence in all aspects of the program, not just an occasional chair test.

Student A	Mon	Tues	Wed	Thu	Fri	Mon	Tues	Wed	Thu	Fri
Reh. Conduct & Participation	20	20	20	20	10	20	10	0	15	20
Perf./Quizzes/Exams	15	100		20	20	15		20	15	10
Running Total	35	155	175	215	245	280	290	310	340	370

Student B	Mon	Tues	Wed	Thu	Fri	Mon	Tues	Wed	Thu	Fri
Reh. Conduct & Participation	20	20	20	20	20	20	20	20	20	20
Perf./Quizzes/Exams	20	100		15	15	20		20	15	10
Running Total	40	160	180	215	250	290	310	350	385	415

As the illustration indicates, after two weeks of instruc- tion, student B would sit ahead of student A, even though both students earned similar performance scores.

Experience has shown that switching chairs once every three weeks for beginners/middle school students and once every nine weeks (or after each performance) for intermediate/high school students works best.

Practice Cards

A comprehensive instructional plan (MAP) negates the need for practice cards. Students should practice for musical achievement, not to satisfy the clock. Weekly performance demonstrations over specific practice material (authentic assessment of music-making) provides meaningful practice goals and real motivation for home practice. Practice cards, on the other hand, frequently serve only to motivate practice time, not practice results.

126

The remainder of this section is a collection of various "success boosters." Each has the capacity to elevate student achievement and enrich a comprehensive instructional plan.

Reward the accomplishment/completion of learning milestones for class work and/or independent study projects.

This can apply to individuals, or better yet, small groups. Teaming is a tremendous means of getting unmotivated students to practice. Cooperative learning with a hint of peer pressure is an extremely powerful motivator.

5th Hour Achievement Chart				Individ. Reward 1	Team Reward 1			Individ. Reward 2		Team Reward 2
Name/Team	Unit 1	Unit 2	Unit 3	Unit 4	Unit 5	Unit 6	Unit 7	Unit 8	Unit 9	Unit 10
Blake (A)	✔	✔	✔	✔						
Darin (B)	✔	✔								
Hannah (C)	✔	✔	✔	✔	✔					
Josh (A)	✔	✔	✔	✔						
Kellie (B)	✔	✔	✔	✔						

Keep individual rewards related to subject matter as much as possible. Save the non-musical perks for team or group accomplishments. Here are a few examples.

✔ *Listening time (bean bags and headphones)*
✔ *Performing a solo with the group accompanying*
✔ *Computer time*
✔ *"Credits" towards going on a field trip to a concert or other musical event*
✔ *Watch a music-related video*

Efficient use of time is directly related to your ability to plan for the lack of it.   **127**

Most experienced teachers have great stories to tell about occasions in which "the students won." You know, those days when nothing was working, the rehearsal just wasn't going anywhere, the students were completely unfocused, and anything that could be considered remotely productive was miles away. Although even the greatest of teachers will have less than perfect rehearsals from time to time, frequent occurrences of this type are more often than not a result of the "fly by the seat of your pants" approach, which is a vicious cycle of these less-than-desirable instructional trademarks:

• *Failing to plan*...thus, planning to fail.

• Playing or singing until a mistake is made...which could have been predicted in the first place. This is also known as the "fix it" approach to conducting.

• Random, frantic drilling of the perpetrator(s)...while the rest of the ensemble sits idle, thinking of a million other places they would rather be. Excluding, of course, those who are too busy passing notes, finishing homework, visiting, or still playing from your last cut-off to notice anyway.

• Mindless repetition...because of *failing to plan.*

In this type of approach, students are cheated out of time, energy, effort, knowledge, and potentially meaningful music-making experiences. In essence, the students pay for our mistakes. Indeed, a truly effective means of turning a rehearsal that is bursting with learning potential into a random string of events is the classic "winging-it" lesson plan. To be more specific, chaotic, unstructured rehearsals are due largely in part to the false presumption that rehearsal planning merely involves jotting down ambiguous things, such as:

Warm-up
Contest tune
Pop tune

As we all know, however, this is more than a little incomplete. Meaningful and progressive learning experiences evolve from thoughtful preparation. Through conscientious planning comes success; without it comes frustration, disorder, and at best, mediocrity. Regardless of the specific musical or instructional context, having a plan—a means to an end—is absolutely mandatory for appreciable and lasting achievement.

Plan ahead. It wasn't raining when Noah built the ark.

Long-Range Planning
Schedule performances: The key is not to schedule too

many, nor too few. Rehearsal time must be carefully reserved for the teaching and learning of meaningful music-making challenges. When too many performances are planned, genuine musical training often disappears to preparation pressure, or cramming. On the other hand, planning too few performances is not advised either. "Coast time" is in reality free time, or "zero-learning time." Interest can only be sustained for so long, and running in place until a performance date finally arrives is an open invitation for discipline problems as well as boredom with music making.

Select music: Finding great music is something that requires considerable attention. On one hand, all of us have our own ideas of what "great" is; musical preference is a very personal thing. On the other, the literature presented to students is the curriculum. Thus, one can only conclude that substantial thought and effort must be given to this task. This takes time and the music-selection process must begin well in advance of the actual learning process. The best educational choices rarely appear from skimming the file cabinet drawer five minutes before rehearsal!

129

Prepare a master calendar: Here are some things not to overlook:

- Performances
- Special rehearsals
- Fundraising drives
- Honor group auditions
- Solo/ensemble events
- Entry deadlines
- Professional development days
- School-wide testing days

- Field trips
- Assemblies

When you're organized, you have time to enrich...innovate...make a difference. When you're unorganized, you only have time to survive.

Short-Range Planning

Score study: The goal here is to get the score in your head so you can keep your head out of the score. By preprogramming your mind with superior musical images (by listening to exemplary recordings and systematic score study), rehearsals become dramatically more efficient and productive as artistic mental images are transformed into artistic sounds. The opposite of this is the all-too-familiar practice of learning the piece "in flight," or at the same time the students do. Simple logic and "caring sense" underscore that this is not the way to go.

> You can't begin a rehearsal without having the score in your soul. You will teach architecture, form, and shape of the piece if you know the score; otherwise, all you teach them is the mechanics, and you will have nothing as a result.[75]
>
> -Larry Rachleff-

Rehearsal plans: Explicit teaching plans arise in the actions of teaching, not a week ahead of time. Thus, lesson plans do not necessarily need to be ultra specific.

The need for clear objectives (which are a direct result of score study), however, cannot be overstated. As Eugene Corporon explains, "great preparation will yield a great rehearsal plan. Our level of achievement is directly related to our mastery of the score, the flexibility and effectiveness of our rehearsal plan, and our ability to communicate."[76] When students clearly understand what they are expected to learn, they are much more likely to actually learn it. Objectives clarify expectations for learning, focus instructional activities, and add precision to evaluation procedures. In Mastery Learning, they further serve as a basis for developing feedback and corrective activities. And as we all know, our world revolves around accomplishment and rewards those who do. If there is no learning or achievement, then we are not really teaching, we are only serving as a glorified baby-sitter.

Creating rehearsal/lesson plans is a task that always sounds worse than it really is. In fact, the process of planning a series of rehearsals is actually fairly simple. Prior to the beginning of each week, or perhaps each performance unit, take a few moments to clarify the musical goals that have been determined through score study. Once this is accomplished, daily lesson plans do not need to be more than a brief outline, or agenda, of what will be done that day towards the accomplishment of your established musical objectives. Of course, if you are compelled to go into more detail with your plans, more power to you. Just be prepared to accept the fact that all rehearsals will not proceed exactly as you had planned.

In a similar vein, the actual task of documenting your plans is something that can easily become just

another thing that "hangs over your head" to do. This,
however, need not be the case. It only takes a simple
form, such as the following, to briefly sketch your
week in advance. Not only is preparing such a document in the best interest of your students' musical
growth, it can be of great benefit to you as well. Amid
the unpredictable pace and schedule of the average
school year, tremendous peace-of-mind comes from
having the foresight to plan ahead.

132

Weekly Planner

Mon	Tues	Wed	Thurs	Fri	Sat	Sun

Musical Goals			Performance Unit	

Daily Rehearsal Plans					Practice Assignments

Announcements

To Do List

Due to the scope and complexity of ensemble training, three primary channels of instruction should be included in the overall program.

Full-Group Rehearsals

Regular rehearsals should be devoted to things that students cannot do by themselves. Anything more than brief breaks to work with small groups or individuals are open invitations for boredom, loss of focus, and discipline problems. After a reasonable period of time, hold students accountable for knowing the "notes and rhythms," or mechanics, so you can keep rehearsals focused on deeper musical issues.

134

Sectionals: The sectional setting offers several advantages:

• The overall quality of a large ensemble performance is highly dependent on each member playing his/her part appropriately. Sectionals reveal students who need one-to-one help and offer a great opportunity to make the necessary scheduling arrangements.

• They provide a relevant environment for learning and applying concepts such as blend, intonation and directed listening, rhythmic precision, and performing with confidence.[77]

• The smaller setting of a sectional allows you to really get to know your students. You can actually visit with them without the rest of the group going crazy.

During the sectional process, it may become evident that a student needs a simplified part. This is acceptable because at least he/she will be performing a part, perhaps completely different than others in the section, but nevertheless, a part. In contrast to fumbling through something too difficult, this allows the student to contribute and experience success.

Sectionals can be held weekly or scheduled on an as-needed basis. Possible times include before school, after school, after lunch, or during "encore" periods. If more than one director is available, holding sectionals during class time is probably the best option.

Master Classes

A sectional can be easily transformed into a master class. This is the perfect setting to address specific things, such as:

135

- Reed making
- The selection and care of reeds or mouthpieces
- Instrument care and maintenance
- The history of an instrument
- Instrument upgrades
- Tone production
- Ear training
- Vibrato
- Articulatory skills
- Diction
- Pitch tendencies
- Special and alternate fingerings
- Transpositions
- Who's who in the world of mezzo-sopranos, flutes, percussion, double basses, etc.
- The performance of music written especially for a particular voice or instrument

Sectionals and master classes should be considered more of a necessity than a luxury. Although the regular rehearsal is where the vast majority of instruction takes place, it is not necessarily the best place to teach all skills and concepts. In many cases, small groups are much more conducive and appropriate.

Teach students how to practice.

When Pablo Casals was 95 years old, a young reporter said to him, "Mr. Casals, you are 95 and the greatest cellist that ever lived. Why do you still practice six times a day?" Mr. Casals replied, "Because I think I'm making progress."

136

Do not assume that students will automatically know how to practice. Effective home practice procedures must be taught and continually reinforced from day one.

■ Teach students a "practice system," such as dividing practice sessions into three segments:

Warm-Up Time: Provide warm-ups for home practice. If left to their own devices, many young musicians will begin their practice session on the highest and loudest notes possible.

Building Time: This time should be spent working on specific practice assignments.

Performance Time: This segment is dedicated to the performance of musical works selected exclusively by the student. Stress the importance of making time for "music that pleases the musician."

■ Reinforce practice procedures by occasionally structuring a lesson or rehearsal to mirror a home practice scenario.

■ Have younger students purchase play-along recordings to accompany them in their home-practice sessions. This makes practicing more fun and provides a
steady tempo to perform with.

Practice on the days you eat.

Make the most of technology.

Technology is unsurpassed as a means of enhancing
traditional modes of instruction. A wealth of information
on how to incorporate technology into the classroom
or rehearsal is just a click away on the internet, and
there are volumes of amazing, user-friendly software
available to boost almost any aspect of musical
development. Granted, it may require a considerable
investment of time, effort, and money to secure the
equipment necessary to make use of technology (com-
puters, keyboards, software, audio equipment, printers,
microphones, etc.), but it is a wise investment indeed.
For example, setting up just one computer station,
complete with notation software and programs for
developing anything from sight-reading skills to ear
training, offers multiple possibilities:

137

• Enrichment work for fast learners
• Corrective work for slow learners
• Independent study projects
• Rewards/Incentives
• Extra credit assignments
• Make-up work

To make "computer time" even more versatile,
provide access to the web and opportunities for

productive use are almost endless. Suffice it to say, a comprehensive approach to music education is incomplete without taking advantage of the many powerful applications of modern technology.

Teach your students the verbal language of music.

There is a vast repertoire of meaningful musical terms and expressions that are open for discovery. This vocabulary represents tradition and purposeful thought that has evolved over hundreds of years. As music educators, we should respect this. It is our obligation to share this vocabulary without transforming or trivializing it.

> A "pick-up" is a truck.
>
> -Frederick Fennell-

> A musician is defined as someone who speaks, reads, writes, and thinks the language.
>
> -Alfred Reed-

Learn as much as you can about your students.

Knowing where your students came from, where they are today, and where they want to be tomorrow is prerequisite to dynamic teaching. A simple question-naire can be a tremendous tool for discovery:

Questionnaire

1. Your name
2. Parent's names
3. Mailing address
4. Home phone
5. email address
6. Instrument/Voice
7. What 3 words best describe you?
8. What are your hobbies?
9. What do you do best?
10. What are you not very good at?
11. Who is one of your heroes? Why?
12. What other school activities are you involved in?
13. What are your career goals?
14. What do you see yourself doing in ten years?
15. What should I know about you so that I can be a good teacher to you?

This information will be kept confidential.

 It is also important to review this information from time to time, particularly when trying to reach a reluctant learner.

Record your students often.

Frequently take the time to allow your students to listen to recordings of themselves. This is a tremendous means of providing non-verbal feedback on their progress, and a prime opportunity to engage them in evaluation, the highest level in Bloom's Taxonomy.

Create special clubs.

For example, form a "sixty-second scale club" where membership is earned by performing all major scales in under one minute. Mark the occasion with a reward, such as a t-shirt or their names engraved on a permanent plaque. Variations of this idea are endless.

Provide students with incentives to participate in non-school related music activities.

A good example is awarding extra credit for attending concerts or reporting on a music- related television special.

Encourage private lessons!

The average tutored student outperforms ninety-eight percent of students taught only under standard classroom group instruction.[78] Any questions?

Establish a "distinguished performer" award.

The criteria for this award can include just about anything. The idea is to simply provide increased motivation to pursue musical excellence.

Example:

• Perform a memorized solo at solo/ensemble festival.
• Audition for an honor group.
• Attend all performances throughout the year.

Remove obstacles.

■ Make it a high priority to teach your students how to properly care for their voices, instruments, reeds, etc. In early stages of instruction, this should be as important as teaching rhythm. Follow this up with routine care/maintenance checks. In terms of preservation, prevention is the best medicine.

■ Make sure that students who play large instruments have a "home horn."

■ Begin a collection of spare instruments that students can borrow during extended repairs.

■ Begin a collection of tuners and metronomes that can be loaned to students.

■ Change is a stressful proposition for many students. Here are a few ideas for easing the transition from one school or group to another:

- *A week or so before enrollment, send each student a professionally- printed invitation to join the next level of the program. This sends the message that the program is not just like any other class, and that membership is a privilege.*
- *Bridge the gap with a joint concert.*
- *Have high school students visit with middle school students to create a "comfort zone."*
- *Assign big brothers/sisters.*

141

■ You can't build up a weakness by hiding it. When faced with a weak section, feature them! Put them in the spotlight and encourage them rise to the occasion.[79]

■ Emphasize top quality mouthpieces, ligatures, and reeds. Improving the point at which the sound begins can make an enormous difference in the consistency and unity of sound within the group, and these cost a lot less than buying all new instruments.[80]

Recruit the assistance of parents.

Encourage parents to listen to their child perform on a regular basis. Point out that this benefits both the student and the program, and can be as simple as listening to their child perform something that he/she had been working on after each practice session.

Explain to parents that there are a number of clues they can look for that give evidence of what's happening, or not happening, in regards to their child's participation in the program. For example, does the child:

✔ *Bring home his or her instrument/music every day?*
✔ *Set aside a specific time each day to practice?*
✔ *Ever talk about the music the class is working on?*
✔ *Practice with friends?*
✔ *Show interest in visiting music stores for supplies, music, etc.?*
✔ *Show concern when absent from a rehearsal?*
✔ *Ever stay after school for disciplinary or non-disciplinary reasons?*
✔ *Use excuses like, "I can perform all of my music perfectly";*
   "We don't have to practice"; "The teacher doesn't like me."

142

All of these clues have something in common. They indicate when or if a student is fully engaged in the program, taking responsibilities seriously, and finding participation enjoyable. If parents perceive there is a problem, encourage them to investigate further and always feel free to contact you.

Compose a visually inviting atmosphere.

Before learning can occur, there has to be a receiving mind. An often under-rated contributor to this is the creation of a physical environment that is conducive to musical teaching and learning. As H. Robert Reynolds (University of Michigan) explains,

The same person will feel (and act) differently, depending on the atmosphere, church, library, gymnasium, home, or rehearsal room. As the sculptors of our surroundings, we must give a lot of thought to cleanliness, the organization of chairs and music stands, what's on the walls, and many other things that take place before a note is played. It's hard to engage in the joy of music making when you don't like the atmosphere.[81]

A visually inviting atmosphere can easily turn a mood from rotten to receptive. Elementary teachers are masters at this. Visit the classroom of a veteran first grade teacher sometime and chances are good that you'll have an "Oh, Wow!" reaction when you enter the room. Here are a few suggestions for transforming your rehearsal room into a warm and inviting "music-making laboratory":

■ Prepare a professional teaching station.
- Raised podium
- Large music stand
- Stool
- Tuner
- Recording deck
- CD/Tape player
- Piano/Keyboard
- Your own instrument(s)

143

■ Emphasize identity and tradition.
- Group pictures from both the past and the present
- Pictures, drawings, or paintings of your school mascot
- Words to your school song and/or alma mater
- Program logo

■ Establish an area where students of today can leave special messages or quotes for the students of tomorrow (a time capsule in progress).

■ Create a "Past, Present, and Future" wall containing pictures, newspaper clippings, awards, etc. Use this to show where the organization has been (accomplishments), where the organization is now (current projects), and where the organization is headed (goals).

■ Establish a special area dedicated to displaying group awards, plaques, and trophies.

When students see awards, plaques, and trophies lying randomly throughout the room collecting dust, what message does this send about the value of these achievements?

■ Create a "Wall of Fame" or "Great Wall of Pride" that honor student leaders, students earning membership in honor groups, and students earning top awards.

■ Don't forget the ceiling.
  • *Flags*
  • *Mobiles*
  • *Banners*
  • *Streamers*
  • *Music-oriented cut-outs (notes, instruments, etc.)*

144

■ Install a map of the United States and add markers indicating all of the places the organization has been.

■ Hang large banners with timely quotes or sayings.
  The spirit of all, the power of one.
  Hours to State Contest...

■ Create a "Positive Board:" a bulletin board where students, teachers, administrators and parents can leave positive notes only. Make it a priority to post at least one note for each student each semester.

■ Install a "Home of the..." sign near your room on the outside of your building.

Teach your students the universal pathway to success.

■ Begin with a vision.

An expanded mind never goes back to its original size.

By asking for the impossible, we get
the best possible.

■ Clarify your goals.
The achievement of goals is success at
the highest level.

■ Determine when your goals will be accomplished.
A goal without a deadline is just a wish.

                    -Jim Irish-   **145**

■ Stay Focused
We are all busy...we all have lives...but
in a successful organization, everyone
makes sacrifices.

He who concentrates upon the task and
forgets the reward may be called man
at his best.

                    -Confucius-

Dance like nobody's watchin'!

                    -Vicki Hannah Lein-

Part of the reward of doing something
is losing yourself in the dance.

-Phil Jackson, *former head coach of the Chicago Bulls-*

Repetition is a means of acquiring success to the smallest detail; it allows
us the opportunity to perfect.

Surround yourself with success. We
become like the people we are around.

It is not aptitude, but attitude that
determines your altitude.

"How does one become a butterfly?" she
asked pensively. "You must want to fly
so much that you are willing to give
up being a caterpillar."

-Trina Paulus, *Hope For The Flowers*-

146

Success is how high you bounce after
you hit bottom.

-General George S. Patton-

The most essential factor is persistence,
the determination never to allow your
energy or enthusiasm to be dampened by the
discouragement that must inevitably come.

-James Whitcomb Riley-

■ Keep growing.
The journey toward the goal is much
more exciting than arriving at the destination.

> Excellence is not a point of arrival, but rather a byproduct of the pilgrimage.
>
> -Dr. Tim Lautzenheiser-

> The reward for a thing well done, is to have done it.
>
> -Ralph Waldo Emerson-

> If you're green, you're growing. If you're ripe, you rot.
>
> -Ray Kroc-

147

Expand your instructional dimensions.

The following are ideas to supplement and enrich the process of preparing a musical work for performance. Comprehensive exploration of great literature not only helps students to perform more artistically, it helps them create a "musical knowledge bank." Occasionally you need to make a deposit so there will always be something to withdraw.

- Listen to other works by the composer; identify related characteristics.

- Invite the composer/arranger to guest conduct.

- Discuss unique customs, lifestyles, etc. of the composers' native country.

- Did the work win any awards? Listen to other works winning the same or similar awards.

- Listen to other works representative of the time period

the piece reflects. Discuss related characteristics.

- Make it a project to compose a short piece of music similar in style to the work being studied.

- When applicable, make it a project to construct a homemade instrument that could be included in the performance.

- Make it a project to write lyrics to the prominent melody of the piece.

- Listen to recordings of other groups performing the work.

- Invite college directors to guest conduct and share their knowledge about the composition.

- Make it a project to create something representative of the period in time that the work reflects or was written. This could range from something to display at a performance to something that could be served at a performance.

Student A performs in an ensemble lead by a conductor whose instructional peak is a mindless repetition of notes and rhythms.

Student B performs in an ensemble lead by a conductor who peaks interest and curiosity with relevant thoughts, facts, concepts, and ideas beyond the notes and rhythms.

Which student were you? Which conductor are you?

Dominant Themes: The Gift of Accomplishment

Teachers have a professional obligation to engineer success. In the realm of music education, nurturing comprehensive musicianship in each individual student is the pathway to accomplishing this task on all levels. For the individual, the process of acquiring musicianship is both a means and an end. Conquering (artistically performing) a sequential series of music-making challenges advances musicianship and brings the music-maker into contact with the internal and external rewards* of music-making. In terms of group accomplishment, the ultimate success of any performing ensemble lies in the musical maturity of each musician. Thus, nurturing the musicianship of the individual is, in essence, nurturing the musicianship of the group. For the educator, a concerted effort to elevate personal musicianship is its own reward. Molding countless students into truly skilled music-makers (in contrast to assembling seat fillers that possess little more than the know-how to perform one part of a small handful of literature) fulfills professional responsibilities, enriches lives, and brings great personal joy and satisfaction. This is real success—accomplishment that infinitely

149

---

* **Internal**: *self-growth, self-knowledge, self-esteem, enjoyment.*
External: *recognition, compensation, respect, support, new opportunities.*

outweighs winning even the grandest of trophies. Short-term gains quickly fade, but long-term investments secure the future. Enjoy the moment, cherish the day.

Comprehensive musicianship does not develop by happenstance. Significant and continuous musical growth requires a comprehensive instructional plan that is based on established principles of effective teaching and learning. A truly effective plan must also be sensitive to the boundaries, time limitations, and hectic pace of performance-based school music programs, and, above all, cater to students on and at all levels. In regards to this, the combination of the following three elements creates a versatile framework for organizing, implementing, and assessing a progressive series of meaningful learning experiences. In other words, an infrastructure for comprehensive musical instruction.

150

I. Class work** based on three interdependent components that each play an indispensable role in attaining superior musical achievement and performances:

- *Conduct & Participation: establishing an environment conducive to teaching and learning.*

- *Music Fundamentals: thorough grounding in key foundations of expressive musical performance.*

** A course of study that learners follow to achieve specific learning goals. In other words, an instructional map that includes summative outcomes, specific learning objectives (mileposts), and instructional activities/strategies that are aligned with established principles of learning and are true to the nature and essence of music.

- *Meaningful Application: the artistic performance of an abundant palette of quality literature that is varied in style and within the students' musical reach.*

II. A realistic plan for encouraging independent study.
Independent study is important because music is so vast. There is so much to learn, explore and discover, yet there is only so much that can be taught within a traditional classroom setting and time frame. Independent study projects give students opportunities to grow at their own pace in directions that are especially interesting or helpful.

151

III. Teaching for mastery.
Mastery learning is important because complete, convincing fulfillment of instructional (musical) objectives is a prerequisite for experiencing the internal and external rewards of music-making, the primary mission of music education. Furthermore, no two students learn in exactly the same way or at exactly the same rate, and it is absolutely essential (understatement) to organize, implement, and assess instruction in a manner which is sensitive to individual needs. The Mastery Learning Model is a powerful force for making this happen.

It should also be noted that a comprehensive instructional plan provides the educator with concrete answers to the following questions:
- *What (exactly) will my students learn?*
- *How (exactly) will my students learn?*
- *How (exactly) will I know?*
- *What (exactly) will be done to maintain and encourage continuous growth in all learners (fast, slow, and all points in between)?*

Although "final answers" must undoubtedly vary as each combination of director, students, school, and program will dictate a somewhat different approach, these issues ultimately determine success.

Teachers who are committed to students and their learning accept, compensate, and prepare for the fact that both music and people are diverse and multi-dimensional. Bringing the two together requires a host of tactics, or "success boosters," that serve to compliment a comprehensive plan of instruction. Things such as taking the time to study scores and prepare rehearsal plans, creating opportunities to work with smaller groups, making the most of technology, encouraging private lessons, and discovering as much as you can about your students (so you can begin on their level and bring them to yours) all raise the potential for achievement and increase the likelihood that students will actually learn that which is being taught.

Whenever educational goals and objectives are achieved (the gift of accomplishment), it is important to emphasize how and why success occurred. Beginning with a specific destination (goals), clarifying the routes of travel, estimating the time of arrival, maintaining a steady pace, and being quick to get back on track after veering off course, are the universal pathways to success, or "means to dreams." Teaching students this truth is just as important as any musical outcome and a trademark of those who truly make a difference.

Success breeds success; accomplishment is addictive. The natural reaction to the internal and external rewards of doing something well is to keep doing it.

153

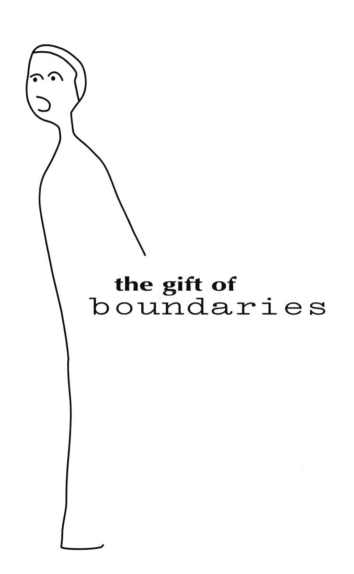

the gift of
boundaries

Although most students would never freely admit it, they really do want boundaries, or behavioral limits. Complete freedom is a scary proposition and many learners fail due to the lack of structure in their lives. A well-managed and task-oriented environment actually comforts students by giving them a sense of order and protection. Structure aids them in becoming more of what they are capable of being. The notion that teachers must win their students over by being "easy-going" is absolutely false. Teachers who set limits and stick to them quickly discover that their students develop a great respect for them. With few exceptions, students need you to be friendly, not their friend.

156

> To educate a person in mind and not in morals is to educate a menace to society.
>
> -Theodore Roosevelt-

> You were hired to take a group of possibly disinterested, howling, and unruly people and turn them into interested, disciplined, and productive learners in a well-managed environment.
>
> -Harry K. Wong-

Teach your students to C.A.R.E.

It's 10:00am and the tardy bell rang 30 seconds ago. While making your way out of your office, you notice Eileen and

Carrie sneaking in through the practice room hallway. As you make your way towards them, you encounter two boys hanging out in a practice room because "they just don't feel like participating today." Torn between which group to deal with first, you are suddenly startled by a loud, shrieking scream from the back of the room. It appears that Katie just had her chair pulled out from behind her. Thankful that there is no permanent damage to Katie or the boy she landed on, you proceed to scold the young man who pulled the stunt. In mid sentence, you are interrupted by Danny, who wants to go to the restroom. Since he asks at the same time everyday, you sense that he really doesn't have to go, but because he caught you off guard, you agree to his request anyway. While finally completing your admonishment over the chair incident, a student runner hands you a request from the counselor to see Shannon. Shannon is not in sight, so you shout out her name. Because of the tremendous amount of socializing that is going on, Shannon, who is in the music library visiting with friends, fails to respond. So you turn to the student runner and say, "She must be absent today." Feeling increasingly stressed, you conclude that it's time to get class started and begin searching for your scores. After rummaging through a few piles, interrupted only by four requests to get a drink, you spot the scores and head for the podium. Upon arrival, you wave your arms frantically, clap your hands a few times, and then shout just a little bit louder than everyone else to finally get the group's attention. It is now 10:15am.

157

This scenario reflects a typical day in the life of a director with poor classroom-management skills. Temporary relief comes from yelling, sarcastic remarks, threats, and random acts of discipline. The solution, however, is to devote considerable attention toward the development of **specific behavioral expectations and rehearsal procedures** that are essential to the success of any school music ensemble. Although this is indeed a tall order, it can effectively be filled by teaching your students to C.A.R.E.

- *Communicate.*
- *Attend all rehearsals and performances.*
- *Respect property and each other.*
- *Execute rehearsal procedures.*

158

C.A.R.E. categorizes specific responsibilities that each student should fulfill on a continuous basis. These responsibilities are prerequisites for effective teaching/learning and help establish an atmosphere that is conducive to the attainment of a crucial goal: rehearsing like a great band/orchestra/choir. Stress that achieving this goal is the key to accomplishing great musical goals. There is simply no other way. Behaviors such as the following have absolutely no place in a great music program:

Inattention
- Talking out of turn
- Constant visiting with friends during rehearsal
- Being unaware of director's instructions

Impulsivity
- Interrupting or intruding on others

- Blurting out comments or questions
- Leaving seat without permission

Oppositional/Defiant
- Being argumentative
- Refusing to cooperate or follow rehearsal procedures
- Deliberately doing things to annoy others
- Blaming others for mistakes or misbehavior
- Acting in a spiteful, vindictive manner
- Sassing without words (dirty looks)
- Commenting disrespectfully (including put downs disguised as a question)

159

Following are examples of personal responsibilities that have proven to be effective in great music programs around the country. Use these as a springboard for creating your own list that is best suited to your personality, degree of tolerance, and specific circumstances.

 The term "rules" has intentionally not been used. Students today have more than enough rules to keep up with, and giving them another set to live by is not the greatest of ideas. Responsibilities, on the other hand, are generally easier for students to swallow and make life so much easier when taught and learned effectively.

Communicate
- *"Call if you are going to be absent."* This is a great way of teaching real life responsibility. Most students will eventually hold a job, and this simple action will be mandatory if they intend to keep it. This also reinforces the team concept by sending the message that absence is a big deal, and that each member performs an important role in the overall success of the organization.

- *"Let me know well in advance about any schedule conflicts."*

- *"If you would like some extra help, just ask. If I can't help you, I'll find someone who can."*

- *"If you are ever troubled or unsure about something that has to do with this program, please come talk to me. My door is always open."*

Attend All Rehearsals and Performances

- *"Be at all rehearsals and performances on time...which means early! There's a difference between being present and being ready."*

160

- *"Being absent from a performance is not like missing a class such as English or History. When even one member of a performing ensemble is gone, the total musical experience is diminished for all."*

Participating in performances should never be perceived as optional. A strict attendance policy is essential; overlooking an unexcused absence sends a conflicting message about the ultimate purpose of a "performance" ensemble. Stress to students that when they sign up for the course they are expected to contribute to each and every performance by being present and putting forth their best effort. Of course, it is also important to provide each participant with a calendar of events as early in the year or semester as possible.

Respect Property and Each Other

- *"Do not touch what is not yours."*

- *"Respect the right of others to learn, and the teacher to teach by not causing an interruption to the rehearsal. Use your good judgment to always know what time it is. Is it time to visit or time to work?"*

- *"Look at the person speaking to you."*

- *"If you cannot say something positive, do not say anything at all."*

Execute Rehearsal Procedures

- *"Be in your seat, ready to make music, by one minute after the tardy bell."*

    If class is first hour and students are "hanging out" in the room beforehand, it is helpful to flash the lights about five minutes before class is to begin. This is their signal to get with it.

161

- *"Do not play your instrument before rehearsal begins."*

    This is key for maintaining sanity and order prior to rehearsal. Try it. You'll be amazed.

- *"Stop immediately when the conductor stops. "*

- *"Raise your hand if you have a comment/question/answer."*

- *"Stay in your seat unless you have permission to do otherwise."*

- *"If you are not able to participate in the rehearsal (e.g. for-got instrument, injured), please see me immediately when you enter the room."*

    Give the student a writing assignment as a means of earning points for the day. This should be done in the regular seat.

    Have the student fill out a form stating his/her name, date, and reason why he/she could not participate. This gives you critical documenta-tion, and even more importantly, lets the student know that you have it.

Name _____

Date _____

I did not participate in rehearsal today for the following reason(s):

_____

_____

_____

Student Signature _____

162

Mail completed forms to parents at the end of each grading period.

- *"Please do not ask to leave class for any reason unless you are ill and need to go home."*

  Although this may seem a bit harsh, when passes to leave the room (restroom, drink, nurse, locker, etc.) are freely given, there will undoubtedly be students who will attempt to take advantage of this...asking to go one place but in reality head for another. Common sense and intuition will tell you when someone really needs to leave the class. Passes to the nurse should only be given if the student is sick enough to go home. If not, he/she will be just as well in the class as in the nurse's office. Restroom passes are more often than not just a free ticket to get out of class for awhile. If a student really has to use the restroom, he/she will make the time in between classes, perhaps even using up a tardy if necessary.

- *"If your instrument is not working properly, please bring it to my attention after rehearsal and I will be glad to help."*

- *"The bell does not dismiss the class, the director dismisses the class. I will do so when the room is in order."*
    - ✓ Chairs and stands in proper positions.
    - ✓ All music put away (so it doesn't look like it just snowed).
    - ✓ Percussion instruments put away.

Timing, consistency, and persistence are crucial when it comes to teaching behavioral expectations and rehearsal procedures. In order for students to perform a piece of music well, it must be rehearsed. The same holds true with procedures. Before a procedure will be performed well, it must be rehearsed. During the first few day of school, devote the vast majority of your time and efforts towards establishing a comfortable, controlled learning environment. Spend as much time as needed until you are absolutely convinced that all students understand their responsibilities. This cannot be stressed enough. Failure to spend adequate time addressing these issues at the beginning of the year is an infallible means of guaranteeing problems through-out the year (about 175 days to be more specific).

163

It is also important to send parents a course syllabus that includes a list of all individual responsibilities that their child is expected to fulfill. Do this very early in the year and include a form to be signed that confirms their understanding of your expectations.

Personal responsibility = the daily fulfillment of behavioral expectations and rehearsal procedures,

or

Personal Responsibility In Daily Effort.

Do not become a "threatening-repeating" teacher.

A sharp tongue can cut your own throat. Students sense very quickly whether or not you will actually follow through on what you say (all bark and no bite). As a professional whose job is to control students under any and all circumstances, it is imperative that you do what you say you're going to do. The way you handle unacceptable conduct and participation must be predictable and consistent. Empty, repetitious threats, such as "one more time and your going to the office," "if I see that happen again you're out of here," "cool it," "knock it off," or "listen up" must be replaced with *swift action*. Not only does this solve the immediate problem, but it deters future problems as well. When students see others actually held accountable for poor choices, they are much more prone to think twice before making the same mistakes.

Examples

✔ Make requests once and only once.

✔ Be everywhere in the room. Stay particularly close to the students prone to cause disturbances.

✔ Whisper Technique: Move close enough to a student to whisper your request. Assume the answer is yes by quickly saying "thank you," breaking eye contact, and moving away. [82]

✔ If a student refuses to cooperate, politely and discreetly tell the student to move to another location that is specifically designated for those who cannot conduct themselves properly. There is simply no valid justification for letting one student bring down an entire group. Situations such as this can be properly dealt with after rehearsal and after the rest of the group has had the benefit of your positive attention.

 Even though you will likely want the disrupter out of your sight, it is a mistake to send a student to a location where he/she is not readily visible.

Do not allow people who cannot control their behavior to control yours.

It takes one fool to talk back. It takes two fools to make a conversation out of it.

-Fred Jones-

165

 Did you really invest all those years in high school, all that money on college, and all those hours in the practice room to spend your career struggling to get students' attention?

Deal with molehills before they become mountains.

The girls in the second row are "social butterflies" and frequently have to be asked to stop talking in rehearsal. They do not necessarily do this everyday, but it does happen quite often.

Angelo, one of the basses in your fourth hour, cannot seem to sit still. He is always fidgety and frequently attempts to leave his seat without permission.

When minor problems such as these appear, be pro-active. For example, arrange for a private, sincere conversation (not a lecture!) with the talkative students. Let them know your feelings on the matter and that you expect cooperation in the future. Emphasize that their actions can only be one of two things: *hurting the group or helping the group.*

In the case of the fidgety student, assigning special hands-on activities to help curb impatience and diffuse excess energy is a much better option than continually harping on the child to be still:

```
"Dominick, please use this metronome to
determine the tempos we are taking in
this piece."
```

```
"Carmine, please use this stop watch to
time the length of each song that we
perform today."
```

More often than not, a little extra attention is all that is required. By taking the time to address minor offenses in a sincere, non-threatening manner, you are supplying a little preventive medicine as well as sending the powerful message that you really are "on their side."

```
A small leak can sink a great ship.
```

In a related vein, it is important to get feedback from students when a problem keeps recurring. Sometimes your perceptions of a problem, or the cause of a problem, might be very different from that of your students. Clearly understanding the views of all parties involved is always a good starting point for preventing and solving problems. An effective means of doing this is to have students write things down. Students are much more open with their thoughts and feelings on paper than they are in conversation.

> The teacher might not be able to play
> as well as you can play; but the
> teacher has thought about how...to get
> the best possible results for longer
> than most of us have been alive.
>
> -Wynton Marsalis-

Rethink your "discipline plan."

How many times have you been in a rehearsal room and seen something like the following:

Discipline Plan
- ✔ Written Assignment
- ✔ One Hour of Detention
- ✔ Two Hours of Detention
- ✔ Send to Principal

167

There are many variations of this, including classics such as the following:

Discipline Plan
- ✔ Number music
- ✔ Dust instrument cases
- ✔ Remove gum from underneath chairs
- ✔ Outta here!

Upon close inspection, "discipline plans" such as these are in reality "punishment plans." They outline things that will be imposed on a student by the teacher for unacceptable behavior or actions. And as Curwin and Mendler explain in *Discipline With Dignity*, this approach to handling problems does not work because...

- They don't teach alternate behaviors.
- They don't generate student commitment.

- They lead to power struggles.
- They attack the students' desire to learn.
- They attack the students' dignity.
- They are inconsistent with classroom learning strategies.[83]

168

Practically speaking, common sense and "caring sense" tell us that a real plan for changing behaviors can in no way be so cut and dry. When discipline problems occur, they are most often a result, or symptom, of something bigger than the actual incident itself: the lack of self-discipline. Thus, what is really needed are not "discipline plans," but rather *"self-discipline plans."*

Instilling self-discipline is a fundamental tenet of education. And like it or not, all educators are presented with many opportunities to deal with this issue almost daily. When faced with a student who is unwilling to follow classroom procedures or fulfill daily responsibilities, educators basically have three options. The first is to ignore the problem completely, which accomplishes nothing. As a second choice, the teacher can fix the problem for the student by immediately doling out punishment. The third option is to work with the students to help them learn how to solve problems by themselves, or from within. By taking this route, problems are not as likely to reoccur throughout the year, or more importantly, throughout the students' lives.

Although the task of teaching self-discipline can be very trying at times, experts on the subject offer many ideas to make the process less stressful for both the teacher and the student. The following four-step approach to handling discipline problems presented by Barbara Coloroso in *Kids are worth it!* is a great place to start.[84]

169

1) *Show the student what he/she has done wrong.* Begin by holding a sincere, one-on-one conversation with the student. Explain your concerns and take the time to listen to theirs as well. It is very important to do this after you have organized your thoughts and are not in the "heat of the moment." An emotional explosion in front of the entire group will only aggravate the problem.

2) *Give the student ownership of the problem.* This step is crucial. By empowering the student to solve problems on his/her own, you are sending a message of trust, which builds self-confidence. Furthermore, the emphasis shifts from external motivation (doling out punishments) to internal motivation (ordering from the inside, or self-discipline).

3) *Help the student find ways of solving the problem.* When a poor choice is made, what the student needs most is a good solution, not a good excuse.[85] Although the student should be allowed "first dibs" on how to solve the problem, a suggestion or two on your part can be very helpful. Chances are you have already been through a similar experience, and it is in his/her best interest to pass this "learned wisdom" along.

> If you blame others for your failures,
> do you credit them for your success?

4) *Leave the students' dignity intact.*
Deal with disciplinary issues in private and attack the problem, not the person. This allows the student to maintain his/her dignity. Public humiliation and verbal assaults diminish self-esteem and imply that the student is the problem, not that the student has a problem that is solvable.[86] Problems with individuals are rarely resolved by addressing them in front of others, especially their peers.

170

Practical Application

Scenario
Beth talks continuously throughout rehearsal. You have explained to your students that during "podium time" there is to be no talking. Realizing that kids are social creatures, you have also explained that during brief "intermissions" in the rehearsal, such as between songs, you will step down from the podium and allow quiet visiting as long as they remain in their seats. Despite this, however, Beth spends most of the rehearsal initiating conversations with those around her.

Step 1
Arrange for a private conversation and let Beth know what she is doing wrong: "Beth, I know you enjoy visiting with your friends, but your continuous talking is causing frequent interruptions in rehearsal. The success of this ensemble depends on teamwork, and this is very distracting to others."

Step 2

Give Beth ownership of the problem: "Beth, I know this is something that you can overcome, and I am going to leave it up to you to solve this problem."

Step 3

Offer Beth options for solving the problem: "I really feel that all you need to do to correct this problem is to think before you speak. You might also try putting a reminder note on your stand. If you're uncomfortable with this, write it in a secret code so that no one else will know what's going on. Another option would be to request to be moved to a seat away your friends."

171

Step 4

Leave Beth's dignity intact: "I know you can handle this Beth. I have great confidence in you, and I'm sure you'll come up with a workable solution."

 The opposite of this scenario would be to abruptly stop rehearsal and say something along the lines of: "Beth, what is it going to take to get you to stop talking in rehearsal?" "Have you no respect?" "One more time and your out of here." Obviously, interrogations such as these do not allow Beth to maintain her dignity. Furthermore, they do not fix the problem.

This four-step approach to handling disciplinary issues takes us a long way from solving students' problems for them, and much closer to providing life changing encouragement and understanding. It gives them an opportunity to exercise positive power in their lives—to live in solutions instead of lying in problems—and sends what Coloroso calls "the six critical life messages:"

1. *I believe in you.*
2. *I trust in you.*
3. *I know you can handle it.*
4. *You are listened to.*
5. *You are cared for.*
6. *You are very important to me.*[87]

Choose your weapons carefully.

The goal throughout the entire process of disciplining students is to teach them that they can make good decisions and solve problems. At the same time, students must also learn that when they make poor decisions, there are often *consequences* to pay. If a person makes the decision not to pay the water bill, and does not respond to the water company's subsequent requests for payment, the water supply will eventually be shut off or disconnected. Likewise, if a student makes the choice not to follow classroom procedures, and is unable to solve the problem on his/her own, then consequences must be accepted.

Consequences should be reasonable and practical; they must "fit the crime" and "fit the student." As nature has it, however, what works with one student will not necessarily work with another. Thus, *being fair does not mean being equal and being equal does not mean being fair.*[88] Consequences should be determined by what will have the greatest impact on a particular student as well as the specific circumstances that surround the incident. In the scenario with Beth, the act of talking is not the main issue. The interruption of the rehearsal is the real problem, and if the problem persists, a reasonable consequence could be to take away the privilege of participating in rehearsal(s) for a predetermined period of time. The ultimate goal is

172

simply to find something that will fix the problem.

Consequences must also leave the students' dignity in tact. As professional educators, our job is to build students up, not tear them down. Mistakes will be made, and many students will make more than their fair share. Dealing with these mistakes in a calm, rational, non humiliating manner is part of your job...it's a "consequence" of being a teacher.

Practical Application

■ Because every child is different and requires a unique approach, think twice before posting a rigid list of consequences. This can pin you into a corner and force you to do something that could very well make a situation worse and fail to solve the problem. If your school requires that you post a discipline plan, use something similar to the following that will allow the flexibility to deal with each situation in a manner that is reasonable, simple, valuable, and practical.

173

1 Warning
2 Conference with a student and director(s) to develop a plan for solving the problem.
3 Consequence(s) appropriate to the behavior(s) or action(s) in question & contact parent(s).
4 Referral to counselor and/or principal.

■ Do not stop rehearsal to deal with minor discipline problems. Simply tell the student to see you after the rest of the group is dismissed. This gets the job done without interrupting the rehearsal and causes minimum loss of face for the student.

■ Here are some examples of practical and reasonable

consequences for typical negative behaviors:

- Wasting the time of others
  Detention

- Being unprepared
  Writing five possible solutions to the problem

- Tardiness
  Being the last to leave

- Interrupting the rehearsal
  Exclusion from class participation

174

■ Once a week, devote an hour or so after school exclusively to improving student behavior. Use this time to contact parents, hold student conferences, send notes or emails, and monitor detention sessions.

Reinforce your offense.

If you sense that a problem with a student is nearing the "consequence stage," it is a good idea to contact the parent(s) and shed some light on the situation.

Practical Application

■ Ask the student to meet you in your office after class.

■ Hand the student the phone and instruct them to call his/her mother or father. Do your best to keep your emotions in check throughout this process. Remember, you are a professional whose job is to deal with anything and everything that the youth entrusted into your care can dish out.

■ Once the parent has been contacted, take the phone and begin the conversation with a kind greeting, and then proceed with: *"I am calling to ask for some advice about how to handle a situation with Molly.* If the situation warrants, you could even continue with something similar to, *"She is right here and I'm going to let her explain the situation to you."*

There are three important advantages to beginning this type of call with a request for advice:

- *It acknowledges that you believe the parent knows the child better than anyone else.*
- *It is free of accusations, which usually puts the parent in a defensive mode.*
- *It gives the parent an opportunity to share wisdom from many years of experience with the child.*

175

Once the conversation gets rolling, it's up to you to keep it focused. Every parent is unique and sometimes things will go great and other times you will hang up feeling that the situation is worse instead of better. By all means, however, never allow a parent to verbally attack you. If things get ugly, do not retaliate. Quickly end the conversation with something along the lines of:

"Mr. Landing, obviously we are not in agreement and I think it's best that we end this conversation now. If you would like to discuss this further, please contact the principal. Good afternoon."

Obviously, your job description does not include enduring verbal assaults from parents who refuse to accept that they were contacted because you were concerned about their child's progress, behavior, or attitude. When parents do not accept or understand that you only want their help so you can best serve their child, you are better off handling the situation without them.

It should be noted that most parent calls do not end in conflict. The vast majority of parents are very grateful for being informed about the progress of their child.

Know when to say when.

Despite everything you may do to bring a problem to a satisfactory resolution, occasionally there will be cases in which a student simply refuses to cooperate. When this happens, it's time to refer the student to the principal with documentation of how you have addressed the situation thus far. This does not mean that it's time to give up on the student, but when the ratio of teacher to students is 100:1, or even 15:1, there will undoubtedly be others that need (deserve!) your attention as well.

176

Love all, serve all.

On a similar note, the ideas discussed here for correcting unacceptable behavior and actions are aimed at normal, everyday types of problems. When faced with major offenses, such as verbal abuse, physical abuse, controlled substances and the like, the best and only choice is to immediately turn the situation over to the principal.

Keep a paper trail.

Document all conversations and steps that you take to resolve disciplinary issues. This will give you great confidence when going into parent/teacher conferences and helps administrators to issue truly befitting consequences when needed.

Scenario

A small group of students cannot seem to "get with the program." They are frequently the last to be ready to begin class, they attempt to visit with their friends continuously throughout the rehearsal, and they are the first to cause an interruption when you are addressing the group with instructions or announcements.

First Time

■ Replace anger or frustration with action; keep the rehearsal on course; using your sensitivity and skill in dealing with others, let the students at fault know that they are to come see you immediately after rehearsal.

177

■ Explain the situation; give them the problem to solve; offer possible solutions; make it a priority to acknowledge any improvement in behavior at the next rehearsal.

Second Time

■ Replace anger or frustration with action; keep the rehearsal on course; using your sensitivity and skill in dealing with others, let the students at fault know that they are to come see you immediately after rehearsal.

■ Remind the students that they have complete ownership of the problem and that it is solvable.

■ Give an assignment that will help reiterate your expectations, such as copying your behavioral expectations and rehearsal procedures five times. This should be signed by a parent and returned on the next school day.

Third Time

■ Replace anger or frustration with action; keep the

rehearsal on course; using your sensitivity and skill in dealing with others, let the students at fault know that they are to come see you immediately after rehearsal.

■ Assign detention.

■ Call or e-mail their parents.

Fourth Time
■ Replace anger or frustration with action; keep the rehearsal on course; using your sensitivity and skill in dealing with others, let the students at fault know that they are to come see you immediately after rehearsal.

■ Refer the students to the principal with documentation of the steps that you have taken to correct the problem.

178

Joseph Alsobrook

Dominant Themes: The Gift of Boundaries

Managing rehearsals with put-downs, yelling and screaming, empty threats or sarcasm is equivalent to treating an abscessed tooth with aspirin. The painkiller will eventually wear off and the problem will be back in full force. Sooner or later, the tooth will have to be professionally cared for. The same holds true for "quick fixes" to discipline problems. Negative displays of emotion and *random acts of discipline* only cause a state of temporary shock. Eventually this will wear off, and discipline problems will continue to occur until they are consistently and professionally dealt with.

179

1. Behavioral expectations and operating procedures must be thoroughly taught and rehearsed. This must be the number one priority of the first few days, or even weeks, of the school year.

2. Do not become a "threatening-repeating" teacher. Be pro-active by reinforcing proper behavior and addressing molehills before they become mountains. Remember the words of a wise batting coach:

"Stand your ground and follow through...follow through...follow through."

3. When poor choices are made, give the student ownership of the problem; encourage solutions, not excuses; share wisdom from past experience.

4. If a problem persists, issue immediate consequences; involve the parent(s). Allow students to maintain their dignity throughout the process.

5. After reasonable attempts to resolve persistent disciplinary issues yourself, refer the student to the principal. There are many others that need your *positive attention* as well.

The Gift of Fun

A leading characteristic of master teachers is their ability to keep the teaching and learning process fresh and unpredictable. No one wants to do the same things day after day, let alone year after year. If students enter the room knowing what's going to happen, you can be sure that they will go on automatic pilot.[89] Once in this mode, they will tune you out and merely go through the motions until you capture their attention with something new. On the other hand, managing students requires a certain degree of consistency, and completely changing the daily routine is not a good idea either. Certain things must always remain the same, such as following classroom procedures and rehearsing like a great ensemble. The happy medium here is to be musically adventurous while keeping the overall flow and structure to your rehearsals constant. *A blend of stability and unpredictability is a recipe for success.*

182

First and foremost, think music!

The single most influential element for making life in your program fun and exciting is found inside your students' folders. Nothing inspires, captivates, or motivates like great works of music. If your students seem bored and disinterested, examine your musical choices. If your rehearsals seem lifeless and ordinary, again, examine your musical choices. Studying well-crafted music that has something say is the fuel for energizing almost every aspect of a school music program. When the right mix of music is programmed, it will seem as if rehearsals end before they even get started. And although the next meeting is just a day away, it will pain you to have to wait for it to finally arrive.

Great music also has a dramatic effect on students. Instead of engaging in feverish visitation before rehearsals, you will notice them actually practicing. They will be significantly more attentive to your instructions and the overall tone of the ensemble will be both cooperative and energetic. Do yourself a huge favor by taking the time, lots of time, to seek out the absolute best music for each of your ensembles. Making life in your classes more "fun" is just one small aspect of the transformational power inherent in all great works of music.

183

The English Literature teacher doesn't use comic books, hoping the students will enjoy the class more.[90]

-Brian M. Olson-

Give your students the VIP treatment.

Variety IP

There are literally thousands and thousands of musical works to choose from. Make it a point *not* to program variations of the same thing every year. For example, there is no law that says a band concert must always consist of a march, an overture, a "slow tune" and a medley of recent pop tunes. Be creative! Make each and every performance an opportunity for your students to experience new types, styles, and forms of music. This is in the best interest of their musical education as well as their sanity. (See also *Diversity,* page 80.)

■ Make sure students have a steady supply of new music to explore. (See also *Study, Performance, and Exposure Works,* page 81-82.)

■ Experiment with non-traditional seating arrangements.
- *Have your students to sit next to someone who plays a different instrument or sings a different part. This offers a completely new perspectiveæsuddenly parts appear that they never knew existed.*

- *Try a circular arrangement. This allows each member of the ensemble to see and hear each other.*

- *Seat students in groups of two or three. This allows for increased proximity control by the teacher and promotes pro-social behavior: every six weeks the students have a new partner to work with, and every class period can begin with a positive greeting to each other. Furthermore, this arrangement allows for pairings of strong-weak, shy-outgoing, disruptive-non-disruptive, and has multiple instructional possibilities:*

  "Let's hear groups one and two play. Group three, you listen for tone quality. Group four, you watch for posture."

  "People on the left play, people on the right check your partner's bow hold and give them some feedback when they're done."[91]

■ Incorporate a song, joke, quote, or saying-of-the-day into your rehearsals.

■ As the performance of a big piece nears, play a recording of the group's first "read through" to demonstrate how far the ensemble has come.

■ Use stand lights for a unique change of atmosphere.

■ Turn off the lights and play something memorized.

■ Customize lessons around current events, such as performing patriotic music in conjunction with a major election.

185

■ As a unique segway into a lesson on how conductors communicate through body language, have your class or a section line up according to their birthdays. There are only two rules: you can't talk and you can't write.

■ **Chamber Music Week:** Divide the group into small multiple ensembles. Each ensemble rehearses on its own Monday-Thursday. On Friday, hold a recital in which each group performs for the class and any invited guests. This also provides a great opportunity to teach concert etiquette.

Breaking students into small groups and assigning them the task of working together to prepare a piece of chamber music is a form of cooperative learning. As Harry K. Wong points out, there is probably more evidence validating the use of cooperative learning than there is for any other aspect of education.[91]

■ **Listening Sessions.** Devote a little time every now and then to listening to a variety of great music. To make these sessions more educational, give your students specific things to listen for during each selection.

Title:
Composer:
Arranger:

List at least 3 specific musical sounds that you hear being performed in this music.

Is this music instrumental, vocal, or both?

Circle the time signatures that you think this music utilizes.

4	3	2	6	2	
4	4	3	8	2	other

Circle the tempo markings that you think this music explores.

Lento   Largo   Andante   Moderato   Allegretto   Allegro   Vivace

List three adjectives that you think best describe this music.

Imagine that you are an "imagineer" for *Walt Disney Company*. In the box below, sketch whatever comes to mind as you listen to this music.

If you were the composer of this music, what would you name it?

You can help students keep an open mind by making comments such as, "This would be a top ten hit in the seventeenth century," or, "If you were alive when this piece was composed, you would think it was cool to wear a wig."

Another effective strategy for keeping students absorbed is to ask them to choose a single word that best describes the piece and then write a short paper justifying their choice.

Listening sessions offer a constructive break from the daily routine that students really enjoy. In fact, it doesn't take long before they start asking to bring their own music to share. You can make a day of it or simply listen to a song or two every now and then. Listening session assignments/journals could even be a required part of student folders. The possibilities are endless, but the value remains the same: exposure to great works of music.

187

Don't expect students to musically "catch on fire" if all they ever get to hear are folk songs, show tunes, or "something-shire" overtures. Was it really just band, orchestra, or choral arrangements that inspired you to make a career out of music?

■ *Music-Around-The-World Week:* Perform or listen to a musical work that is representative of a different country on each day of the week.

■ *Daily sight-reading:* Not only do regular sight-reading sessions develop musical skills, but they also expose your students to a "diverse musical palette."

■ Keep an electronic keyboard handy for musical examples, sound effects, etc.

■Repetition allows us the opportunity to perfect...
but keep it interesting! For example, the initial
performance of a song/exercise in a method book
is essentially sight-reading, so treat it as such.
Afterwards, subsequent performances can be made
more interesting and constructive through any of the
following strategies:

- *"Pulse" the rhythms. For example, a dotted quarter note would be performed as three eighth notes.*

- *Alternate performances between a soloist (or section) and the full ensemble. Assuming the soloist is the director or a talented student, this is a tremendous means of creating superior musical images for the group to imitate. Instrumental students can also "air-play" during the soloists' turn.*

- *Give special directions, such as, "This time I want you to leave out the fourth beat of each measure and replace it with a rest," or, "Leave out eighth notes when they follow dotted quarters."[92]*

- *Say/sing the note names.*

- *Ask students to raise their hands if they would like to pick a song to be played by the full group. Once selected, the student should say the title (or number) out loud...but only once so that the rest of the group is forced to listen. After a song has been chosen, give them a five-to-ten second countdown to find the piece and prepare to sing/play. Students love this!*

- *Addition/Subtraction. Begin an exercise with the entire class and add/subtract one section upon each repetition.[93]*

Monotony is probably the conductor's
biggest enemy.

-H. Robert Reynolds-

V Involvement P

Kids want action. Keep them actively engaged in music making for as much of the rehearsal as possible.

Tell me and I'll forget...show me and
I'll remember... but INVOLVE ME, and
I'll understand!

189

■ **Continuous Play:** As the ensemble nears the end of an exercise or a section of a piece that you are rehearsing, call out the name of a specific group. For explanation purposes, let's assume you select "woodwinds." When the full group reaches the end of the selection, the woodwinds will then immediately, and in tempo, repeat the selection. As the woodwinds near the end of the passage, another group is called upon which follows suit.

By selecting any of the groups listed below, endless variations of this rehearsal strategy are possible.

• Individuals
• Duets
• Trios
• Sections (sopranos, altos, trumpets, flutes, cellos, etc.)
• Parts (1st, 2nd, 3rd, etc.)
• Choirs
• Rows
• Girls/Guys

- Classes (Freshman, Sophomores, etc.)
- Chairs: (all first chairs, all second chairs, all third chairs, etc.)

Advantages to using the continuous play strategy:
- Keeps students alert and attentive because they never know which group you are going to pick...it just might be them.
- Allows for multiple repetitions of a section without wearing everyone out.
- Isolates individuals, sections, groups, etc. so you can really determine "who's got it" and who doesn't.

190

■ When it becomes apparent that a section or group needs some work that will probably take a while, come up with a way for everyone in the ensemble to help. The goal is for no one to sit idle for more than a few seconds. For example, if the trumpets were having a rhythm problem, the rest of the group could get involved in several ways:

- Write the rhythm pattern in question on the board. After counting, play the rhythm pattern (as a group) on a unison pitch.
- Trumpets play the part while the rest of the group performs basic rhythmic pulses underneath.
- Trumpets play the part while the rest of the group counts the rhythm.
- Trumpets play the part while the rest of the group claps the rhythm.
- Alternate between the trumpets playing the actual part and the rest of the group playing the part on a related unison pitch.

VIPace

Staying in one gear for too long is a sure-fire way of losing interest. Watch a couple of music videos, or spend a few minutes playing a video game, and you will quickly discover the fast-paced, ever-changing world that students are used to.

Do not stop and spend several minutes of full rehearsal time working with individuals or small groups. Full group rehearsals should be spent predominantly on full group practice. Try to keep stops under thirty seconds. Use sectionals to address section problems and tutoring sessions for helping individuals. If this is not possible, take a rehearsal or two and work with students needing assistance while the rest of the ensemble does a written assignment. This is far more productive than spending day after day working with students who need extra help while the rest of the group sits (impatiently) waiting for them to "get it."

191

Get acquainted with what your students are interested in.

You don't personally have to love it, just accept it. In the eyes of 7th graders, for example, if someone wrote a song called "Who's going out with who, who can whip who, video games, sleeping in, and chocolate," it would become an instant hit. The point is to simply find out what your students are *into* and incorporate this *into* your instruction.

- Have students fill out questionnaires early in the year (see page 139).
- Seize every opportunity that presents itself to visit with your students, such as on bus rides. Be inquisitive:

   What do you enjoy doing in your free time?

Where do you and your friends hang out?
Why?
What was the last CD you purchased?
What radio stations do you listen to?

Be crazy!

✔ Use good-humored nicknames.

✔ Participate in school wide "dress-up days."

✔ *Surprise your students with something completely unexpected.* For example, I once hired a local ice cream truck to drive through the middle of a marching band rehearsal on a hot August afternoon. Of course I made sure that the driver would proceed very slowly and have that annoying little tune they play cranked as loud as possible. Once the truck was in the middle of the practice field, the driver got out (amidst the perplexed looks from all the students) and shouted "You guys look like you need some free ice cream!" Needless to say, it was a hit. Here are some other examples to help stimulate your creativity:

> ✎ *Show up to rehearsal wearing a completely unexpected outfit, such as a costume characteristic of the 1700's, to accentuate your study of Mozart.*
> ✎ *Play a practical joke.*
> ✎ *About a week before a major performance, pass out a bite-size candy bar to your students as they leave with a note attached that says, "Beginning tomorrow, it's CRUNCH time!"*
> ✎ *Incorporate recorded audio blips from radio, TV, or movies to add a unique twist to your lessons.*

✔ Give each student a welcome package on the first day of school. Some possible things to include are:

✎ *Course syllabus/handbook*
✎ *A gift certificate to a local music store*
✎ *Discount coupons to a local record store*
✎ *Pencils*
✎ *Calendar/Day Planner*
✎ *Sample of an upcoming fundraiser (candy bars, magazines, etc.)*

> Conformity is the jailer of freedom and the enemy of growth.
>
> -John F. Kennedy-

193

If you think back to when you were in school, it is likely that some of your fondest memories are of occasions that came with great anticipation. Not only does having something to look forward to make us happy, it is a great motivator for reaching higher levels of achievement because it provides a sense of purpose and direction to our efforts.

When planning performances, let creativity and imagination be your guide.

• Program a musical work that involves a guest artist/soloist.

• Program a musical work that involves a guest narrator (administrator, TV personality, football coach, etc.).

• Invite a guest to conduct a piece on the concert. How about a local musician, a retired director, the actual composer, or the town mayor?

- Hold your concert in conjunction with another event, such as an art show or a craft fair.

- Organize a combined concert with all music groups in your school or district.

- Have a small reception after the concert with refreshments. This is great "PR" time.

- Plan something for stage changes.
  - ✎ Soloists
  - ✎ Small ensembles (duets or percussion ensembles work well for this)
  - ✎ Comments from the president of the booster organization
  - ✎ Videos

- Premiere student compositions. Let the student composer conduct the piece if he/she desires.

- Invite alumni, or family members who are capable, to join the group for a performance of a song that has special meaning to your program or school.

- Premiere a new composition (commissions).

- Give your concert a theme.
  Examples
  - ✎ Patriotic
  - ✎ Celebration of the child
  - ✎ Pops
  - ✎ Cartoons
  - ✎ Space music
  - ✎ Movie music
  - ✎ Sea songs
  - ✎ Evolution of Jazz
  - ✎ Music of a certain composer
  - ✎ Journey through the classics

✎ *Name those tunes*
✎ *Music of a specific historical period*
✎ *Music of a specific musical style*
✎ *Music from around the world (use plane tickets for programs)*
✎ *Ticker Tape Parade (music characteristic of groups passing by in a parade)*
✎ *Best of...*

- Establish your own "signature songs" and perform them on the last concert of the year.

- Create special medleys using short segments of popular (not necessarily "pop") and favorite songs. Incorporate exceptional vocalists or instrumentalists, costumes, acting, magic, dancing, narration, special lighting, sound effects, jokes, props, etc...the sky's the limit! Students always have great ideas for these and can be very helpful in putting them together.

195

- Have students memorize a short grand finale tune. Play this song with the students out in the audience.

- Hold a candlelight concert during the holidays.

- Try a "Concert in the Round" (table seating around the ensemble).
    ✎ *Make the place mats the concert program.*
    ✎ *Cover tables with butcher paper and set out some crayons.*
    ✎ *Put musical jokes on place mats.*
    ✎ *Create centerpieces related to the program or concert.*
    ✎ *Serve goodies such as pie, cake, cookies, candy canes, etc.*

- Hold a benefit concert for a local charity or shelter.

Cover charges
  ✎ Canned goods
  ✎ Toys
  ✎ Pet food
  ✎ Used clothing/coats

- Always include student names in your printed programs. Without names, programs have no keepsake
  value to students or parents. Here are some other
  things that could be included as well.
      ✎ An article about the history of
         bands/orchestras/choirs in your community
      ✎ A short history of the school or program
      ✎ Student quotes about how music or the program
         has influenced their lives
      ✎ A "did you know" section with statistics and/or
         information about the program or the values of
         music education
      ✎ An article about, or from, the booster organization
      ✎ A letter from a school administrator
      ✎ Quotes about the values of music education
      ✎ Information about the composers
      ✎ Information about the musical works
      ✎ A copy of a vintage concert program from the
         same group
      ✎ A vintage picture of the group
      ✎ The words to the school song

   In the last printed program of each year, list each
student's *cumulative* music related accomplishments
next to his/her name. If the ensemble is very large, you
could limit this to students who are graduating or
moving on to another school. For example:

Erika Martin *(Senior)*
Choir member for seven years; All-District Choir member, four years; All-State Choir member, two years; District Solo/Ensemble Contest: 11 Superior ratings and four Excellent ratings; State Solo/Ensemble Contest: seven Superior ratings; Choir President, 1999-2000; "Laurie" in *Oklahoma,* Spring musical 1999; "Liza Doolittle" in My Fair Lady, Spring musical 2000.

 You could also list the cumulative program accomplishments for the entire tenure of the graduating class.

197

Broaden your performance horizons!

Students need a steady supply of varied and ambitious performance goals to look forward to. This allows them to experience the satisfaction of accomplishment and boosts the amount of energy they put into the preparation process. Flash! This does not come from the following scenario:

Begin the year with a little of this and a little of that, throw together a Christmas concert because the holiday is suddenly only two weeks away, spend three months drilling two contest tunes (three if students are lucky), perform a couple of pop songs for a Spring concert, and then kill time until school finally(!) lets out.

Keeping in mind that every performance doesn't have to be an elaborate production, just enough to keep students working with a purpose; why not try something new? In addition to regular concerts, consider including some of these performance locales and opportunities in your performance calendar.

Contests
Festivals
Retirement homes
Charity balls
School assemblies
School sports events
Professional sports events
Town fairs and celebrations
Parades
Grand openings
Naturalization ceremonies
Graduation ceremonies

198

Inaugurations
Music conventions
Send offs
Art shows
Rotary/Kiwanis/Lions club meetings
Booster meetings
Faculty meetings
Parent/Teacher Association meetings and events
School board meetings
Town meetings
Charity fund raising events
School bond issue watch parties
Local television programs
Local malls
City parks

"Sweeten the pot."

Although praise and encouragement will always be the best form of positive reinforcement, here are some additional things that can done or given to recognize extra effort, a series of great rehearsals, special achievement, etc. Please do not confuse this with bribery. It is only natural for students to enjoy looking forward to an *occasional* perk in recognition of their hard work and efforts. These things are harmless, and the increased motivation they provide over-compensates any negative aspects.

Donuts
Sodas
Candy Bars
Order in lunch from a local restaurant
Patches
Lapel pins in the shape of a music note or instrument
Computer time
CDs
Headphones and CD time (you provide the CDs!)
Limousine rides (go out to lunch and then cruise around town)
Fifteen seconds in a "Money Bin" (many fundraising companies have these)
Small pillows marked with the program logo
Gift certificates to a music or record store
Lunch out after a festival or contest performance
Pizza party
Ice cream sundae party
Movie and popcorn party

 Delegate a party organization. Students are incredibly skilled at such things.

Publish a "reader-friendly" newsletter.

In addition to the basics (dates, reminders, etc.), include fun things such as music-related jokes, timely quotes, and the results of student polls. This could also be posted on your web site.

Examples

Favorite musical work performed so far this year
Best song of the year
Best movie of the year
Favorite soda
Favorite CD
Favorite TV show
Favorite musical artist
Favorite color
Best burger in town
Best pizza in town
Best place to go on a date
Favorite video game
Favorite book

200

At first glance, some of the ideas in this section may seem a bit impractical (and certainly non-musical). However, they are included for good reason...they were born out of the mouths of students. For example, the foregoing ideas stemmed from asking my students what it would take to get them to actually read my newsletters. It was a very busy time of year and there was a great deal of information that I wanted them to remember. Despite all of my efforts to document this information, many students were oblivious to it. Sure, everyone received a newsletter, but very few took the time to read it. When I jazzed it up with more than just "boring old stuff," however, my students took a whole new interest in it. Indeed, it is crazy, harmless things such as this that can sometimes make a huge impact. Furthermore, and for reasons unknown to adults, these things can help mold a group of very different students with very different backgrounds into a united musical family.

Capture life in your program on film.

If you really want to make a stir, start taking pictures.

The photos you take can be of just about anything,
e.g. entering the room, rehearsing, performing, just
hanging out, etc. The content is really not important.
Students simply love to look at pictures of themselves
and their friends. Curiously, this has a bonding effect
in addition to being just plain fun.

 For a unique wall decoration, create a "Family Tree" using various pictures of each student in the group.

Invite an out-of-the-ordinary musical act to perform for your classes:

- Barber shop quartet
- Bagpipes
- Alp horns
- One-man-band
- Electronic music demos (keyboards, drums)
- Steel drum ensemble

Have fun with holidays:

- Perform patriotic songs on Veteran's Day.
- Perform love songs or go serenading on Valentine's Day.
- Perform spooky music on Halloween.
- Perform Irish tunes on St. Patrick's Day (do this, and leprechauns will dance for you).
- Play an April Fools Joke.
- Have parents and student leaders organize a holiday party.

Hold an end-of-the-year banquet.

Include a slide/video show that recaps the year. Make
sure at least some of the background music includes

songs that the students performed themselves.

     ✎ Incorporate pictures/videos of upperclassmen when they were beginners.

     ✎ Decorate with a theme.

 Banquet organization is another great project to delegate to students and parents.

Instead of wasting time on the last few days of school, do something fun and constructive.

- Play or sing through every song that your students have learned since the beginning of the year. This is a great way to emphasize how much the group has accomplished. To make this successful, give your students the year-long project of maintaining a folder that is complete with each and every piece of music that you have given them. After this "year in review," each student should turn in their folder for a grade.

- Make up musical games based on popular TV game shows. Make sure the content is related to materials that were learned throughout the year.

- Hold a chamber music recital: Ask each student who performed at a solo/ensemble event to perform for the class.

- *Listening sessions (See page 186)*

- Have an award ceremony in which you and your students present serious and humorous awards to each other. Screen these ahead of time to weed out any awards that "cross the line."

Appeal to your students' sense of adventure by embarking on a performance tour.

Trips do not have to be an annual occurrence. Students will be content as long as they get to take at least one "major" trip before graduation. Here is a list of things that can help make your trips more successful: [95]

• Before agreeing to let a travel company make your trip arrangements, ask for references and contact the Better Business Bureau in the state where the company is located. Have there been any complaints filed against them?

203

• Contact the Federal Trade Commission at www.ftc.gov for reports on travel company fraud and misrepresentation as well as information to guide you in choosing and using a reputable travel company.

• Get approval from the school administration *before* telling students and parents about the trip.

• When planning overnight trips, recruit enough parents/sponsors so there is one in every room. Book a hotel that has a suite-type layout, and you can have four students and one sponsor in each room. Book a hotel that has adjoining rooms, and you can have six students and one sponsor in each unit. This takes a little more effort to organize, and it probably will cost a little extra, but the number of hassles and headaches it saves is more than worth it. No walking the halls at night and students never go unsupervised.

• Plan a full schedule of fun and educational activities. Excessive free time equals trouble.

• Several weeks before departure, let everyone

involved know the dates of travel, itinerary, accom-
modations, luggage limitations, dress code, costs
involved, etc.

- Establish a clear-cut cancellation policy.

- Hold at least one parent meeting for trips longer
  than a weekend to provide specific information on
  the itinerary and supervision. Be prepared to answer
  questions such as the following:

  - *Who are the adults going on the trip?*
  - *Where will my child be, and what will my child be
    doing throughout the trip?*
  - *How can I be sure that my child will be safe?*

- Provide specific written details for students and parents that include names, places, emergency numbers, daily schedules, roommates, etc.

- Provide students with a checklist of things to bring.
  Along with the basics, don't forget the following:

  - *Calling card or pre-paid phone cards*
  - *Quarters for pay phones and vending machines*
  - *Sunscreen*
  - *Sunglasses*
  - *Saline solution for contacts*
  - *Inhaler, prescription medication*
  - *Things for the bus ride:*
    Movies
    Snacks
    Bottled water
    Blanket & pillow
    Homework
    Personal CD player with headphones

- Require all students to submit a signed, notarized

medical release form that includes emergency contact information.

- Check with your district's legal counsel to be sure that all liability issues are covered.

- Make arrangements for chaperones to have cell phones to use in case of emergency.

- Cover emergency procedures with all students participating (e.g. what to do if you get sick, what to do if you get separated from the group).

- Establish a *trip hotline* that is updated daily by a designated parent on the trip. Parents at home really appreciate being able to call and get an update on how things are going.

205

- When spending the day at a theme park, establish specific times and locations for students to check in. It is also helpful to have parents take shifts by the first aid station.

Dominant Themes: The Gift of Fun

Keeping the teaching/learning process fresh and exciting generates energy for music making. A combination of stability and unpredictability, or being musically adventurous while maintaining the overall flow and structure of the class, is the pathway to accomplishing this.

The most influential factor for keeping music-making exciting is music itself. Making the rehearsal process more fun is just one of several advantages to offering students a diverse palette of truly great musical literature.

Variety, Involvement, and Pace are prime elements, or building blocks, for engineering and implementing rehearsals that are both fun and constructive. Giving students the VIP treatment is key to avoiding typical rehearsal problems, stimulating participation, and waking up minds.

In addition to stirring enthusiasm, giving students something to look forward to boosts achievement because it gives purpose and direction to their efforts. Anticipation is motivation in an exuberant form.

Complimenting traditional modes of instruction with unique performance opportunities, unexpected surprises, and occasional perks and adventures enriches the overall teaching and learning process. Transforming the ordinary into the extraordinary is a potent formula for sustaining interest, building a united musical family, and enabling more students to experience the many values of formal music instruction.

208

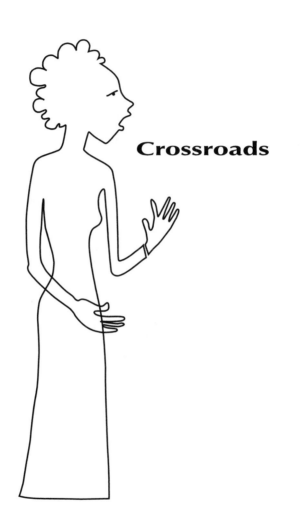

Crossroads

The Gifts of:

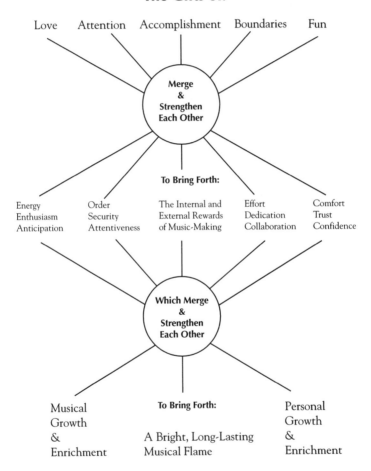

Love   Attention   Accomplishment   Boundaries   Fun

Merge & Strengthen Each Other

To Bring Forth:

Energy	Order	The Internal and	Effort	Comfort
Enthusiasm	Security	External Rewards	Dedication	Trust
Anticipation	Attentiveness	of Music-Making	Collaboration	Confidence

Which Merge & Strengthen Each Other

To Bring Forth:

Musical Growth & Enrichment   A Bright, Long-Lasting Musical Flame   Personal Growth & Enrichment

This book only begins to scratch the surface of the many ways that a giving approach can energize a school music program. The fundamental human aspirations that this text addresses are versatile building blocks for developing healthy relationships and effecting positive change. The gift of accomplishment, or success in learning, should naturally be the centerpiece of your efforts. It is the root from which all other gifts will grow and is the ultimate mission of any educator. At the same time, however, without the gifts of love, attention, fun, and boundaries, truly successful teaching and learning, by any stretch of the imagination, is next to impossible. In other words, each gift plays an important and unique role in bringing forth lasting growth and enrichment. It is the loving and unconditionally accepting teacher who allows students to take risks and explore their potential without the fear of humiliation or rejection. A musical learning environment that is fun and exciting wakes up minds and causes students to look forward to each new venture with great anticipation. The creation of boundaries builds a bridge of respect between teachers and students while establishing an atmosphere conducive to discovery and retention. And to strengthen the overall relationship between teacher and learner, the gift of attention is unsurpassed and feeling needed and valuable is motivation in its purest form.

In essence, giving is a way of thinking, limited only by your imagination. Thus it is by no means a period, but merely a pause. Giving is a lifelong process that separates one from the masses; makes the mundane magical, and energizes the mind, body, and spirit. Perhaps most relevant, however, is the fact that giving is a dynamic instrument for bringing students from all walks of life in touch with the joys of music. It is the pathway illuminating music as a gift with never-ending gifts to share.

212

As long as there are students in search of love, fun, confidence, attention, and success, there will always be a need to give...which is exactly how I would like to conclude this book. Underlying all of the thoughts, ideas, and strategies that embrace these pages are four interconnected messages that summarize the cause, effect, and importance of a giving approach to music education. They are, in fact, the real "secrets" to bringing out the best in students and making the most of your career. Consider these principles as guides in the quest to *understand before being understood* and as mileposts along the journey to become a life enriching band, orchestra, or choir director.

The world we have created is a product of our thinking; it cannot be changed without changing our thinking.

-Albert Einstein-

Although superior personal musicianship is irreplaceable, it takes many other special qualities to be a truly effective, life- enriching music director. You must be as compassionate as you are steadfast in your determination to hold students accountable. You must be as unpredictable as you are consistent. You must be as creative as you are competent in established principles of effective teaching and learning, and you must be as flexible as you are structured. In short, you must be a multi-dimensional giver. It is people—unique, multi-dimensional creatures—who make music, and you must be prepared to compensate for the fact that what works with one student will not necessarily work with another.

213

Life is a test. It is only a test. Had this been a real life you would have been instructed where to go and what to do.

Look within. If your program is everything you always dreamed it could be—an exemplary model of personal and musical achievement—it is because you made it that way. If your program is not, you must look within. It is not the students', parents', or administration's fault, it is yours. Real success comes from continuously giving to others, from going above and beyond that which is required, from a far-reaching extension of yourself. As the captain of your ship, *you* must change before the program will change. In the words of L. Dale Barnett, a wise friend and colleague,

"Kids are kids! Lead and they will follow...follow and they will lead."

You reap what you sow. If you want to get more out of your students, give them more of what they want most. If you want more involvement from your parents, get more involved with your parents. If you want more cooperation from your co-workers, be more cooperative with your co-workers. If you want more support from your school, get out and support the school. It's that simple. What comes around goes around, and the internal and external rewards received from teaching are directly proportional to the amount of personal energy that you invest in giving to others.

Giving is its own reward. It is both a pathway and a destination.

It only takes a spark to ignite a brilliant flame. Without even knowing it, you could very well change the course of a student's life, not only by your words and actions, but through your belief that the student can achieve and succeed. Like it or not, you play a dual role as a school band, orchestra, or choir director. In addition to building performance skills, you are building character; in addition to shaping phrases, you are shaping attitudes; and in addition to helping your students realize musical goals, you are helping them to realize their potential. The magnitude of this charge is awesome and the challenge before you is immense. You can choose to make a difference—to be enriched by enriching lives—or you can choose to be indifferent, and let living, breathing opportunities pass you by.

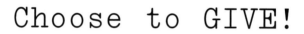

Choose to GIVE!

End Notes

1. Luann Fulbright, "Give Instructions Students Can Follow," *Better Teaching* 13.15 (7 April 2000): p. 2.

2. Judith Delzell, "The Location of Students and their Equipment." As quoted in *Teaching Techniques and Insights,* revised edition by Joseph L. Casey. (Chicago: GIA Publications, Inc., 1993): p. 390.

3. These comments and ideas were quoted from Ruby K. Payne in *A Framework For Understanding Poverty* (Highlands, TX: RFT, 1998), pp. 48-49.

4. Gary Zukav, *The Seat Of The Soul* (New York, NY: Fireside, 1989), pp. 225-226.

5. Will Schmid, "The Performance Challenge," *Music Educators Journal* 82.6 (May 1996): p. 4.

6. Eugene Corporon, "After Four Years." As quoted in *Teaching Techniques and Insights,* revised edition by Joseph L. Casey. (Chicago: GIA Publications, Inc., 1993): p. 27.

7. Eldon A. Janzen, *Band Director's Survival Guide* (West Nyack, NY: Parker, 1985), p. 78.

8. David J. Elliot, *Music Matters* (New York, NY: Oxford University Press, 1995), pp. 133-134.

9. Quoted from the Oklahoma Secondary Schools Activities Association "Music Regulations Manual," 1999-2000.

10. *Ibid.*

217

11. Tim Lautzenheiser, "Standing United As We Agree To Disagree," *Fanfare* 9.1 (February 1996): p. 12.

12. Dale Carnegie, *How To Win Friends & Influence People* (New York, NY: Pocket Books, 1981), p. 124.

13. Barbara Gross Davis, "Motivating Students," *www.uga.berkeley.edu/sled/bgd/motivate.html.*

14. Carol S. Dweck, "How Can Teachers Develop Students' Motivation - And Success?," *Education World* 1.1 (April 2000): p. 12.

15. Bryce Taylor , "Dynamics." As quoted in *Teaching Techniques and Insights,* revised edition by Joseph L. Casey. (Chicago: GIA Publications, Inc., 1993): p. 228.

16. Harry K. Wong, Rosemary T. Wong, *The First Days Of School* (Mountain View, CA: Harry K. Wong Publications, Inc., 1998), p. 76.

17. Tim Lautzenheiser, *The Joy of Inspired Teaching* (Chicago: GIA Publications, Inc., 1993), p. 83.

18. Dale Carnegie, *How To Win Friends & Influence People* (New York, NY: Pocket Books, 1981), p. 177.

19. Richard Carlson, *Don't Sweat the Small Stuff: and it's all small stuff* (New York, NY: Hyperion, 1997), p. 21.

20. Tim Lautzenheiser, *The Joy of Inspired Teaching* (Chicago: GIA Publications, Inc., 1993), p. 85.

21. *Ibid,* p. 87.

22. Quoted from a *Motivational Message Card,* author unknown. Celebrating Excellence, 919 Springer Drive, Lombard, Illinois, 60148.

23. See the December 1995 issue of the *Instrumentalist* magazine for a great example of this.

24. David J. Elliot, *Music Matters* (New York, NY: Oxford University Press, 1995), p. 130.

25. Eugene Corporon, "The Quantum Conductor." As quoted in *Teaching Music through Performance in Band,* Compiled and Edited by Richard Miles. (Chicago: GIA Publications, Inc., 1997): pp. 25-26.

26. Harry K. Wong, Rosemary T. Wong, *The First Days Of School* (Mountain View, CA: Harry K. Wong Publications, Inc., 1998), pp. 255-256.

27. "Congress Champions Music Education," *School Band and Orchestra* 3.4 (April 2000): p. 6.

28. As quoted in "Profiles of SAT and Achievement Test Takers," The College Board, compiled by the MENC, 1995.

29. Ross A. Leeper, "Memorizing." As quoted in *Teaching Techniques and Insights,* revised edition by Joseph L. Casey. (Chicago: GIA Publications,1993): pp. 15-16.

30. *Professor Walter Fields,* Video Tape, Mark Scharenbroich, Scharenbroich & Associates, 2000.

31. Tim Lautzenheiser, "Standing United As We Agree To Disagree," *Fanfare* 9.1 (February 1996): p. 11.

32. Harry K. Wong, Rosemary Tripi Wong, *The First Days of School* (Sunnyvale, CA: Harry K. Wong Publications, 1991), p. 123.

33. Kirk Kassner, "Motivation for Instrumentalists," *Music Educators Journal* (May 1987): p. 51.

34. Eugene Corporon, "The Quantum Conductor." As quoted in *Teaching Music through Performance in Band,* Compiled and Edited by Richard Miles. (Chicago: GIA Publications, Inc., 1997): pp. 22-23.

35. David J. Elliot, *Music Matters* (New York, NY: Oxford University Press, 1995), p. 60.

36. Will Schmid, "The Performance Challenge," *Music Educators Journal* 82.6 (June 1996): p. 4.

37. Daniel L. Kohut, *Instrumental Music Pedagogy: Teaching Techniques for School Band and Orchestra Directors* (Englewood Cliffs, NJ: Prentice-Hall, Inc., 1973), p. 217.

38. David J. Elliot, *Music Matters* (New York, NY: Oxford University Press, 1995), p. 119.

39. *Ibid,* p. 119.

40. *Ibid,* p. 115.

41. *Ibid,* p. 129.

42. *Ibid,* p. 122.

220

43. Robert C. Rawlins, "Practice Should Be Fun, But It Must Involve The Mastery Of Realistic Goals," *LeBlanc Bell XX*.1 (Winter 1997): p. 16.

44. H. Robert Reynolds, "Guiding Principles of Conducting," *BD Guide* 7.4 (March/April 1993): p. 5.

45. Thomas R. Guskey, *Implementing Mastery Learning* (Belmont, CA: Wadsworth Publishing Co., 1985), p. ix.

46. *Ibid,* p. xiii.

47. *Ibid,* p. xi.

48. *Ibid,* p. xx.

49. Harry K. Wong, Rosemary Tripi Wong, *The First Days Of School* (Sunnyvale, CA: Harry K. Wong Publications, 1991), p. 215.

50. H. Robert Reynolds, "Guiding Principles of Conducting," *BD Guide* 7.4 (March/April 1993): p. 4.

51. Eugene Corporon, "The Quantum Conductor." As quoted in *Teaching Music through Performance in Band,* Compiled and Edited by Richard Miles. (Chicago: GIA Publications, Inc., 1997): p. 13.

52. Richard Floyd, "Expressive Playing." As quoted in *Teaching Techniques and Insights,* revised edition by Joseph L. Casey. (Chicago: GIA Publications, Inc., 1993): p. 31.

53. H. Robert Reynolds, "Painting by the Numbers." As quoted in *Teaching Techniques and Insights,* revised edition by Joseph L. Casey. (Chicago: GIA Publications, Inc., 1993): p. 24.

221

54. Daniel L. Kohut, *Musical Performance: Learning Theory and Pedagogy* (Englewood Cliffs, NJ: Prentice-Hall, 1985), pp. 5-7.

55. *Ibid*, p. 10.

56. *Ibid*, p. 23.

57. *Ibid*, p. 11.

58. *Ibid*, p. 14.

59. H. Robert Reynolds, "Two Ways To Learn." quoted in *Teaching Techniques and Insights,* revised edition by Joseph L. Casey. (Chicago: GIA Publications, Inc., 1993): p. 14.

60. Daniel L. Kohut, *Musical Performance: Learning Theory and Pedagogy* (Englewood Cliffs, NJ: Prentice-Hall, Inc., 1985), p. 17.

61 Barry Green with W. Timothy Gallwey, *The Inner Game of Music* (Garden City, NY: Anchor Press/Doubleday, 1986), p. 16.

62. *Ibid*, p. 17.

63. *Ibid*, p. 24.

64. *Ibid*, p. 47.

65. *Ibid*, p. 134.

66. *Ibid*, p. 136.

67. *Ibid*, p. 136.

68. Thomas R. Guskey, Implementing Mastery Learning (Belmont, CA: Wadsworth Publishing Co., 1985), p. 7.

69. Scott A. Stewart, "The Middle School Factor," *School Band and Orchestra* 3.1 (January 2000): p. 53.

70. Quoted from Harry K. Wong during a professional development workshop in Bartlesville, Oklahoma.

71. Thomas R. Gusky, *Implementing Mastery Learning* (Belmont, CA: Wadsworth Publishing Co., 1985), p. 131.

72. Edwin Kruth, "Performance Standards," *BW 2001* 16:3 (January-February 2001): p. 10.

73. Adopted from an *Audience Behavior Rubric* in "Assessing a Cast of Thousands" by Patricia Chiodo, *Music Educators Journal* 87.b (May 2001): p. 21.

74. James Croft, "Planning for Rehearsals." As quoted in *Teaching Techniques and Insights,* revised edition by Joseph L. Casey. (Chicago: GIA Publications, Inc., 1993): p. 379.

75. Larry Rachleff, "Score Study." As quoted in Teaching Techniques and Insights, revised edition by Joseph L. Casey. (Chicago: GIA Publications, Inc., 1993): p. 375.

76. Eugene Corporon, "The Quantum Conductor." As quoted in *Teaching Music through Performance in Band,* Compiled and Edited by Richard Miles. (Chicago: GIA Publications, Inc., 1999): p. 16.

77. Daniel L. Kohut, *Instrumental Music Pedagogy: Teaching Techniques for School Band and Orchestra*

Directors (Englewood Cliffs, NJ: Prentice-Hall, Inc., 1973), p. 217.

78. Harry K. Wong, Rosemary T. Wong, *The First Days Of School* (Mountain View, CA: Harry K. Wong Publications, Inc., 1998), p. 243.

79. Robert E. Foster, "Motivating a Weaker Section." As quoted in *Teaching Techniques and Insights,* revised edition by Joseph L. Casey. (Chicago: GIA Publications, Inc., 1993): pp. 50-51.

80. Terry Austin, "The Henry D. Thoreau Intermediate School," *Young BDGuide* 1.1 (Spring 1993): p. 10.

81. H. Robert Reynolds, "Guiding Principles of Conducting," *BD Guide* 7.4 (March/April 1993): p. 5.

82. Quoted from a presentation by Sylvia Lowe, Aim High: Setting High Expectations for Your Students (A Preventive Discipline Plan).

83. Richard L. Curwin, Allen N. Mendler, *Discipline With Dignity* (Washington, D.C.: Association of Supervision and Curriculum Development, 1989).

84. Barbara Coloroso, *Kids Are Worth It!* (New York, NY: Avon Books, 1984), p. 29.

85. *Ibid,* p. 106.

86. *Ibid,* p. 106.

87. *Ibid,* p. 27.

224

88. Richard L. Curwin, Allen N. Mendler, *Discipline With Dignity* (Washington, D.C.: Association of Supervision and Curriculum Development, 1989).

89. Michael Kaufman, "Predictable and Unpredictable Rehearsals." As quoted in Teaching Techniques and Insights, revised edition by Joseph L. Casey. (Chicago: GIA Publications, Inc.,1993): p. 45.

90. Brian M. Olson, "A Challenge for Young Band Conductors," Young BDGuide 1.2 (Fall 1993): pp.10-12.

91. Scott A. Stewart, "The Middle School Factor," *School Band and Orchestra* 3.1 (January 2000): p. 52.

92. Harry K. Wong, Rosemary T. Wong, *The First Days Of School* (Mountain View, CA: Harry K. Wong Publications, Inc., 1998), p. 254.

93. Ross A. Leeper, "Increasing Concentration and Accuracy." As quoted in *Teaching Techniques and Insights*, revised edition by Joseph L. Casey. (Chicago: GIA Publications, Inc., 1993): p. 167.

94. Trey Reely, "Creative Repetition for Beginning Band Classes," *Bandworld* (October-December 1996): p. 10.

95. Many of the ideas for making trips more successful were taken from "School Trips" by Mary Jo Patterson and Lyn Fiscus. Quoted in the National Association of Student Activities *Advisor Brief* (Reston, VA: National Association of Secondary School Principals, 2000).

225

About The Author

I am a messenger. My message is music, my mission is enrichment.

I am a molder of unspoken thoughts, a shaper of phrases, a first aid techni-cian, and a cheese and sausage salesman.

My favorite colors are red and black. They used to be red and white. Before that they were blue and gold.

I am saddened when my students go...most of the time. There are so many that I will never forget, and I often wonder what they will become.

I believe that my students are capable of achieving amazing things. Many times they manage to learn in spite of me.

I have traveled all over the country and seen many spectacular sights...but never without students, and always on a bus.

I know that secretaries really run schools, and I know where to find the custodians at any time of the day or night. I do not understand why I have more keys than they do.

My office was originally designed to be a closet...it also serves as the library. Next to the aspirin in my desk drawer are sticky notes, a few bandages, lots of safety pins, and a wrench for tightening music stands. I am always out of tissue.

I rest just as comfortably on grass as I do on turf.

I know that teaching music is a snap...after I have figured out how to unite the diverse, ever-changing personalities that my students are blessed with.

I will never understand drummers...or cymbal knots...or extra-duty stipends.

I can convince 200 parents to sell a truckload of fruit...tonight. I cannot convince them to pick up their children on time. I can convince 100 students to show up for a 5:30am rehearsal. I cannot convince them to remember a pencil.

I am very attached to the phrase, "What was I thinking!" Another favorite is "Why?" There are many days in which the school bell is music to my ears.

I believe the greatest students I'll ever have are here today and gone tomorrow...the same was true yesterday.

My sons understand words like paradid-
dle and purchase order. Their wardrobe
is part trendy fashion, part school
T-shirts.

I know that great works of music can
nourish the soul...almost as much as
ice cream.

I am certain that I could make more
money doing something else, but I will
remain steadfast on this path. For it
is music...and students...and knowledge...and family that I hold as treasures.
And when I am old and gray, rocking on
my front porch, my memories of life
will be rich.

Just like you, I have chosen to give.

I am your brother.